Saving
Susie-Belle

Saving Susie-Belle

RESCUED FROM THE HORRORS OF A PUPPY FARM,
ONE DOG'S UPLIFTING TRUE STORY

JANETTA HARVEY

JOHN BLAKE

Published by John Blake Publishing Ltd,
3 Bramber Court, 2 Bramber Road,
London W14 9PB, England

www.johnblakepublishing.co.uk

www.facebook.com/Johnblakepub facebook
twitter.com/johnblakepub twitter

First published in 2014

ISBN: 978-1-78219-752-2

British Library Cataloguing-in-Publication Data:

A catalogue record for this book is available from the British Library.

Design by www.envydesign.co.uk

Printed and bound in Great Britain by CPI Group (UK) Ltd

3 5 7 9 10 8 6 4 2

Papers used by John Blake Publishing are natural, recyclable products made
from wood grown in sustainable forests. The manufacturing processes conform
to the environmental regulations of the country of origin.

Every attempt has been made to contact the relevant copyright-holders,
but some were unobtainable. We would be grateful if the
appropriate people could contact us.

John Blake Publishing is not responsible for the content or views
found in any external source given in the book.

In affectionate memory of my friend
Elizabeth Ries who loved Jasmine and would
have adored Renae and Susie-Belle

Author's Note

In sharing Susie-Belle's and my story I hope to highlight some of the dreadful practices that go on in the cruel world of puppy farming. It is a frustration that for legal reasons I have had to be less forthright than I would like in places but if you would like to know more and find out what you can do to help end puppy farming please read my blog at http://susiefoodie.blogspot. co.uk/ or follow me on twitter @SusieBSchnauzer or on Facebook at https://www.facebook.com/pages/Susie-Belle-Schnauzer/705830289434936?ref=hl

Contents

Introduction   xi

Chapter One   Love Struck   1
Chapter Two   Reborn   11
Chapter Three   Spotting Susie-Belle   21
Chapter Four   Amongst the Misfits   33
Chapter Five   Susie-Belle's First Day Out   41
Chapter Six   What's in a Name?   51
Chapter Seven   Nocturnal Dramatics   61
Chapter Eight   Crowds and a Cool Dip   71
Chapter Nine   Not All Dogs Like a Stroke   81
Chapter Ten   Susie-Belle Finds Her Voice   91
Chapter Eleven   Food Glorious Food   101
Chapter Twelve   Reunion   111
Chapter Thirteen   Tasty Sights   119
Chapter Fourteen   Sunday in the City   131
Chapter Fifteen   Susie-Belle Arrives in France   141

Chapter Sixteen   **No More Skinny Susie-Belle**   153
Chapter Seventeen   **Up and Down**   161
Chapter Eighteen   **A Stormy Night Under Canvas**   171
Chapter Nineteen   **Swimming Buddies**   181
Chapter Twenty   **Growing Expectations**   189
Chapter Twenty-One   **Dragged Backwards by a Clip**   197
Chapter Twenty-Two   **Fruit Salad Days**   205
Chapter Twenty-Three   **Courage Rewarded**   217
Chapter Twenty-Four   **Learning From Susie-Belle**   223

Acknowledgments   233
Further Reading and Information   235

Introduction

'If you pick up a starving dog and make him prosperous, he will not bite you. This is the principal difference between a dog and a man'

– PUDDN'HEAD WILSON, *MARK TWAIN*

In the week before Christmas, on a bed beside a log burner in a house in England a dog with a belly full of lobster snoozed. A few months earlier that dog had lain in the cold and filth of a puppy farm, her belly empty of food but full with her last litter of puppies. For six years she had been trapped in a life of misery as someone's commodity – a puppy farm breeding bitch, tied up in the back of a putrid shed, never seeing the outside world, receiving little or no care, experiencing neglect to a horrifying degree. Producing puppies, that's something she must have been good at, for if not, she would have been dispatched, most likely shot. On leaving her particular hellhole she would have been missed by no one, never knowing that life can be good.

Ironic that in being good at the task, her continuing fertility condemned her to more years of cruelty than if she had been a failure. For she remained profitable all the while her thin, abused body produced the goods. Only when her babies stopped coming would she be allowed to rest in peace, however that arrived. For this little dog, peace came before death, for she is one of the lucky ones – that is, if we regard surviving years of loneliness, pain and terror as being lucky. For she was rescued, lifted out of the dark and grubby hidden nightmare that is puppy farming and brought to safety into our world. Now she shares our peaceful home and experiences nothing less than complete loving daily care. Where once she was a scabby, nameless creature, now she has a beautiful name, and for my miniature schnauzer Susie-Belle life these days is good, as good as it can possibly be. Never again will it be anything less for this gentle soul who has suffered at the hands of humans who value commercial profits more than life itself.

Susie-Belle had been living with us for four months when she experienced her first ever Christmas outside of the puppy farm. During that time, she had gone from being a timid, bald, thin little creature to being a slightly less timid, a lot less bald, plump little pet. She arrived with a voracious appetite. Her timidity temporarily faded at mealtimes and we indulged her in ways that would exceed most people's expectations of good food. Susie-Belle ate every meal like it might be her last and for a dog that had until recently known what it was to feel the pain of starvation, why would she not? In those first weeks with us, she experienced not only the sweet taste of freedom but delicious meals of venison, rabbit and hare plus delectable morsels of roast goose and some of our now legendary pre-Christmas lobster. For Susie-Belle survived starvation and neglect to find herself loved, protected and in a home of indulgent foodies.

In our house my husband Michel, a professional chef and culinary wizard, conjures up meals to delight and nourish all those under his roof, pets most definitely included. Susie-Belle had landed in foodie heaven, where the damage from her previous hell could be gently healed and with time would eventually be forgotten. For us food is a joy we share with our friends and family and in our home, our pets are family. We have owned miniature schnauzers for most of our married life and have always taken the view that if we are to bring dogs into our lives, then we must really live together as joyfully as they deserve, not just casually cohabit the shared space. We see that we must care for them as well as we care for any other family member and share all the good times we can provide.

With us, mealtimes are never functional affairs, there's mindfulness about how we prepare and enjoy food. We strive to eat healthily and well and most importantly we love doing so, whilst respecting the wise words of Hippocrates,

Let food be thy medicine and medicine be thy food

Our philosophy with food is simple: it must be tasty and healthy and good to share and we have never seen any reason why our pets cannot be included in this. When Susie-Belle arrived in August 2011 she was so damaged that it was the most natural thing in the world for us to seek ways to help her heal through food. Diet is the fundamental way to promote good health and this is as true for animals as it is humans. In our frenetic modern lives, it is easy not to really give what we feed our pets much thought, though. But in our home food is one of our most thorough pleasures and our dogs thrive on what we do for them. That's not to say they eat the same as we do, but they eat equally well. Many a time over the years friends have commented that our dogs eat better than some humans.

I work in the natural health field and I've spent a long time understanding the nutritional needs of both humans and dogs. To provide a dog with a healthy diet, I know that a reasonable depth of knowledge is needed, along with a generous pinch of common sense. When I say we indulge our dogs, they are indulged through top nutrition with careful thought and planning. They're not given food that is wrong for them, they are given food that the wonderful animal humans love and live with needs. *Canis lupus familiaris* (the domestic dog) has managed to survive and thrive long before the advent of modern commercial food manufacturing. It's easy to feel that we cannot feed our pets well without relying on commercially prepared foods; all those tins and packets of complete dog food weighing down shelves in supermarkets and veterinary practices surely means that by doing it ourselves, we risk doing it wrong and without the correct approach that would be right. However, the American food writer Michael Pollan's take on food in his book, *In Defence of Food*, is one that resonates with us and one we find as relevant to feeding our dogs as it is to ourselves,

> *Don't eat anything your great-great grandmother wouldn't recognize as food. There are a great many food-like items in the supermarket your ancestors wouldn't recognize as food... stay away from these.*

INTRODUCTION

So we home prepare meals for our pets and Susie-Belle, we soon discovered, is our perfect culinary companion. She will eat virtually everything we offer her and with such unmistakable pleasure that she delightfully quivers from nose tip to tail when a favourite dinner is served. For any dog owner, this would be a wonderful thing to see but, in Susie-Belle's case, every single time it is a heart-melting sight and we never cease to be warmed by her joyous reaction. The frail, emaciated, severely damaged dog that came out of hell with very little life left in her bravely set aside her fears and by allowing herself to trust the humans with whom she was fated to live the rest of her life, she has embraced the life of a true canine gourmet. What is even sweeter is that she shows us daily how good it makes her feel and this is no mean achievement on her part as she spent years never knowing how to communicate anything but fear. Not all dogs that come from the type of background Susie-Belle has can show delight in food. Some are so traumatised after years of having to fight for scraps that they cannot eat normally when they go to live in their adoptive homes. Whether Susie-Belle was always a canine gourmet without the opportunity to know it, or whether living with foodies has created this we shall never know. What matters is that we have found a way of bringing her joy on a daily basis, something we heartily believe she has richly earned.

Miniature schnauzers are traditionally thought of as being alert, intelligent, tough companion dogs, and Susie-Belle had spent the last six years in horrendous confinement, producing puppy after puppy after puppy. Twice a year in a relentless cycle of enforced mating she would have whelped a litter of babies to satisfy the commercial demands of the rough end of the puppy trade. Although the mass commercial production of dogs is commonly called 'puppy farming', I believe this lends a cloak of respectability and benign animal husbandry to an industry where greed, cruelty and abuse that no normal thinking person would recognise as farming is endemic. Factory, or battery farming of puppies is a more accurate way to describe this. For many thousands of years dogs have been companions to humans and for me this sits uneasily with the idea of puppies as livestock. In the United States, the term 'puppy mill' comes close to the reality of the merciless cycle of mass production that puppy farming represents.

The mass commercial production of puppies purely for profit to be traded and sold to dealers, or via the unscrupulous masquerading as legitimate breeders, gives no thought to the welfare or happiness of the parent dogs or pups. Typically, they are kept in dark, horrific conditions, often in wire cages, sometimes stacked on top of each other – meaning the dogs lower down are left to live amongst the excrement falling from above, as well as their own filth. On rescue, dogs that have lived their entire lives in these cages typically have splayed toes from standing on wire floors. If not in cages, small, cramped concrete pens are used, where no bedding and little food is provided and any water is dirty. Derelict agricultural buildings are commonly turned into dog factories and often granted planning permission then run as entirely legal businesses, which is disturbing to most people I talk to. Some are illegal, but nevertheless remain in business, flouting regulations, continuing the misery; making money for those behind them.

The dogs held in these places have little contact with humans and certainly never experience any love or tenderness. They are roughly manhandled, grabbed at, kicked out of the way and caught in doorways by their heads or bodies, should they try to escape. The ratio of humans to dogs is pitiful; some puppy farms have been found to contain several hundred dogs, managed by only a couple of people. The poor creatures are totally unsocialised, have multiple health and behavioural problems and, for females like Susie-Belle, many have hernias from prolonged, painful labours. Most of them live out their years riddled with infection, in pain and never seeing daylight, let alone being taken for a walk. This has lasting effects on how they move through life if they are ever rescued and have the chance, like Susie-Belle, to live in normal homes. Their puppies are taken away very young, as early as five weeks. These pitiful creatures are often poorly, some with congenital diseases from the inbreeding that is common. They are then sold online, in pet shops or in free classified ads and many die soon after being transferred to their new homes. For the few adult dogs to leave these places alive, once they are rescued, they leave having been severely traumatised for their entire life; they have no experience of living in a normal home and as a result they are extremely frightened and confused.

Through the work of those courageous, dedicated animal rescuers who are prepared to go into these grisly places, Susie-Belle was saved. She was found in the back of an agricultural shed, tied up with rope about her neck and taken to safety by people who work to persuade commercial puppy producers that there are homes that their worn-out dogs might 'retire' to rather than be shot because they are no longer productive. These rescuers have their critics, though. There are those who believe that in taking the spent breeding animals off their hands, the rescuers assist the farmers, in some way colluding with the whole dirty business. I disagree with this viewpoint because the dogs like Susie-Belle that are being cleared away are the ones who would otherwise be killed, being no longer productive.

Whether the dogs are taken by rescuers, or killed by the person confining them, their space will be taken by a successor, quite possibly one of their own pups. The rescuers offer these discarded, broken breeding machines the chance to live out their lives in peace, lives that one way or another would otherwise be over. It was from this background that Susie-Belle emerged and it is the story of our time together during her first year of freedom that I share here.

CHAPTER ONE

Love Struck

'You think those dogs will not be in heaven! I tell you they will be there long before any of us'

– ROBERT LOUIS STEVENSON

I was vaguely aware that the battery farming of puppies goes on when we bought our first dog, a miniature schnauzer we named Jasmine, several years beforehand. However, with chagrin I know in all honesty that I never gave it a tremendous amount of attention. Like many people, once we had decided getting a dog was a good idea, we did a sketchy bit of research and went to a breeder within easy reach. Our research was guided largely by my boss at the time's keenness on schnauzers and after reading up on them a miniature schnauzer seemed an ideal choice for our first dog. Choosing Jasmine was as simple as going to the first breeder I found. I vaguely knew that a puppy should be seen with its mother and be interacting normally with both its mother and littermates, which should also be available for viewing. I had all this in mind when I went with my boss to choose my first ever puppy, but beyond that I was pretty ignorant of what I should be looking for.

We arrived at the breeder one hot August afternoon, driving into a large yard with a row of wooden sheds running along the perimeter fence. As soon as we got out of the car, the breeder came from the house and casually greeted my boss, who explained that I was there to pick a schnauzer. Simple as that, no searching questions from me to confirm that the breeder was breeding to high standards or following good practices. No requests to see certificates of health screening of parents and puppies. Nor were there any questions from the breeder for me as to what sort of life I was going to provide for the puppy. No, it was as easy a transaction as buying a bag of sugar. More exciting and expensive for me, but just as mundane for the seller of schnauzer puppies that day. How things would change for me a few years down the line when the full reality of what I was helping to support that hot afternoon hit home.

The breeder confirmed she had puppies available and without much further ado went into one of the sheds and brought out a couple of the most gorgeous, fluffy faced puppies imaginable. Of course all puppies are cute, but schnauzers really do have the most adorable appearance. With bright little eyes and cute envelope shaped ears, they resemble spiky bottle brushes. Up to that point in my life, I hadn't seen many puppies and who doesn't find a tiny, helpless pup irresistible, let alone someone with their heart set on buying a puppy that day? It was a done deal as soon as the breeder placed the tiny ball of grey fluffy life in my hands. I vividly remember holding Jasmine for the first time, nervously wondering how to relate to this fragile bundle of fur when she quickly dealt with any developing neuroses on my part by tilting her head to one side and giving my cheek the gentlest of licks. I was smitten. Just before my newly besotted brain went into total meltdown from the effects of having an adorable puppy's head tilt and lick away any trace of common sense I just about managed to ask where Jasmine's mother was. 'Busy in the house with her pups' was an answer I remember and one I thought no more about, being utterly overwhelmed by the joy of having a puppy in my arms who clearly, or so I like to think, wanted to come home with me. It was only later when I remembered that Jasmine had not been brought from the house, she had appeared from one of the sheds.

My boss was of the view that Jasmine wasn't the right puppy, that she was too docile, too quiet and gentle, and that I should go for her more boisterous sister, who was busy nibbling away at his shirt collar, wriggling in his arms and squeaking with excitement. But Jasmine's charm had worked perfectly on me, as it would continue to do her entire life, and nothing would change my mind. She was my choice and I was hers and little would shift me from my decision. Not even the passing pangs of concern that I felt over not seeing her mother or the guilty discomfort when I looked across the yard and saw multiple wooden tubs containing Westie and Yorkshire terrier puppies clamouring for attention in the sawdust lined tubs. Despite having done a little homework and knowing this didn't seem a happy way for pups to be kept, I turned my back and a blind eye and duly wrote out the cheque for Jasmine.

I will never know for certain what Jasmine's true origins were, whether she was bred there on-site as I was told from healthy, happy parents, or if she was bought in from a puppy dealer and traded from those premises. My thoughts these days are that Jasmine was probably, although by no means certainly, bred there, in one of the numerous wooden sheds. There were several adult schnauzers running free and seemingly happy in the yard; they were friendly and looked well cared for. They were probably the breeding stock of the breeder or unsold puppies awaiting the start of their breeding life. As for breeding to healthy standards and having certificates to prove that the requisite health screening had been done, I do not know if any of this would have entered the mind of the breeder. I also don't believe that the Westie and Yorkie puppies were bred on site – they were numerous and I did not see any adults around. Keeping them in the barrels for buyers to pick out like potatoes on a market stall leads me to believe that they came from a farm elsewhere.

As I have come in recent times to understand the full horrors endemic in the dirty end of the commercial dog breeding world, I have wrestled a lot with my conscience. Whilst I felt uncomfortable at seeing the puppies out in the sun in tubs, I still pushed those concerns aside as I had fallen instantly in love with my chosen pup. Like many other puppy buyers I was daft. Coupled with the convenience of it being hassle free, not having to sit on a breeder's waiting list for months on end, this all served to snuff out any remaining twinges of conscience which may have led me to walk away with my cheque unwritten. I cannot change what was done, all I can do is hope that by sharing what I now know, others may not repeat my mistake as I take heed of Oscar Wilde's wise words:

To regret one's own experiences is to arrest one's own development. To deny one's own experiences is to put a lie into the lips of one's own life.

Whilst Susie-Belle was trapped in misery, we enjoyed a full and active life with Jasmine for fourteen and a half years. From the quietly charming puppy grew a lively, noisy, fun-loving female who enjoyed doing everything we involved her in, which was soon almost everything we did. Many a time I was thankful that I had ignored my boss and gone with the quieter puppy choice, as my quiet puppy soon became an energetic live wire, forever on the lookout for the next activity, the next person to pester, the next dog to rough and tumble with. Jasmine was great fun and hard work in equal measure for the first few years of our life together. As novice owners, we made many mistakes in the early years and failed spectacularly at ever getting her to control her insatiable need to bark at everyone and every dog we met whilst out and about. Miniature schnauzers have a reputation for their noisiness and Jasmine didn't let the side down. Indeed she well and truly lived up to that reputation. Locally she was renowned as the dog who talked to everyone: she barked away at dogs over the other side of the park as she ran across to them to invite them to play, she barked at children across the road to let them know she was there; she barked at anyone we met out and about who didn't give her the attention she desired quickly enough. I was once told that if I tried to shush her with words, she would just think I was barking along with her. I think they were right. The more we tried to quieten her down, the more she thought we were joining in her conversation and up the noise level would go.

But we took comfort from the fact that other dogs seemed to understand her, and never did her noisiness get her into any canine trouble – the dogs got our Jasmine, the same couldn't always be said of the humans. We took advice from many sources, some of it good advice, a lot of it nonsense, and we could get none of it to work. With hindsight, we now know that we were not consistent in anything we did with her and would be somewhat sporadic in how we tried to address it as we found her vocal character pretty amusing a lot of the time and it soon came to define who she was. Of course what we found a quirky, often embarrassing trait, not everyone found so charming and there were occasions when I wanted the ground to open up for Jasmine and me as she barked her way along a busy high street. But the responsibility lay with us. We didn't have the knowledge or experience to know how to properly manage her vocal reactivity and over the years, we just muddled through with the training, bumbled along enjoying our lively outings and all in all, gave her the best life we knew how to whilst growing thicker skins along the way.

Jasmine steadily became central to how we structured our days, months and years. Through our many years together we discovered just how much happiness there is on offer when we allow dogs to truly share our lives. From the outset we wanted to have a dog that would travel with us and participate in all things completely. We gradually organised matters so that we could include her in almost everything we did. Anything we couldn't include her in soon faded from our lives. As soon as the British government relaxed the rules on allowing dogs to travel in and out of the UK by introducing the Pet Travel Scheme in 2001, we bought a second home in southwest France so that we could enjoy spending time there with Jasmine. Up to that point in her life, we had only holidayed in the British Isles, preferring not to leave her out of the fun of holidays. By the time of her death in 2010 Jasmine had made well over a hundred trips across the Channel and spent around four months every year there enjoying its charms. We took her through the stunning Ardèche valley one year, and another year stayed with friends in the Alpes-de-Haute-Provence. There she came along with us when we visited fragrant lavender fields and temporarily lost her voice wandering in the busy summer markets of Provence, too distracted by the smells, sights and sounds to voice her opinion. She trustingly joined us on hikes along trails to remote mountain villages and forgave us for foolishly taking her out all day in the sun on one memorably hot summer day's hike.

Up until she was 10 years old, Jasmine's health was robust and largely problem-free, which is far from always the case with many puppies from uncertain breeding. We used to meet another dog out on our local walks that came from the same place and he died horribly young, having been ill on and off for much of his short life. Sadly this is all too common an outcome when breeding standards are of no interest but commercial ones reign. Then, at 10, Jasmine's cruciate ligament ruptured in her right knee and she had to undergo major surgery. At the same time, it was found that she had hip dysplasia, a genetically passed on malformation of the hip joints inevitably related to her parental background, the details of course unknown. This, together with the knee operation, took its toll and although she recovered well from the surgery and continued to enjoy several more years of relatively good health, from that time on she noticeably entered her veteran years. Her activity levels declined and finally, after all those years, her infamous excitability calmed itself. We never thought we would miss her loudly announcing herself to everyone in the park, but as she moved into old age, her barks grew increasingly fewer, her running more sedate and her bed became the place where we would find her more and more.

In her final few months it became increasingly clear that we were on limited time with the wonderful friend who had shared so much with us and for more than fourteen years had been the centre point and source of much joy in our lives. As her zest for life faded it became obvious to everyone that she wasn't going to be with us for much longer. People close to us who had known her for a very long time gently whispered about life post-Jasmine. Would we get another dog? I couldn't bring myself to discuss openly the painful reality of her being old and frail and grappled with unbearable sadness at the realisation that we would have to face life without this magnificent character who had by now in her twilight mellowed into the sweetest, gentlest old lady imaginable.

We did everything we could to make her last months with us as comfortable as they could be. Apart from arthritic issues, and an obvious slowing up and lower energy levels, she didn't appear to suffer any illness and still displayed a fine appetite and enjoyed regular outings. She was on an assortment of prescribed medicines, supplements and herbs recommended by our UK and French vets. To ease her aches and pains she had regular massage and acupuncture and we ensured she enjoyed a peaceful home and restful times whenever she wanted them. Where once she had happily walked several miles a day, it was now all she could do to plod with us the five hundred yards over to the park and back. Her physical world shrank as her vitality dimmed but she still insisted on getting out each day to see her pals in the park. Of all the puppies and dogs that we had met and known throughout her lifetime, she now reigned as the *grand dame* of the park, the only surviving member of her original peer group. So many dogs had passed on, many younger than her. Many times it hit me that for those of us who live with and love our pets the greatest sadness is that their time with us is always far too short.

During her last trip to France in the autumn of 2010,

Jasmine seemed to gain a temporary new lease of life, walking a little further each day than she had managed in a very long time. We had a friend staying with us who couldn't believe she was the same dog that we had, with heavy hearts, warned might not make the holiday should her health take a turn for the worse. She must have thought we were making it up when we said that we believed ourselves to be on borrowed time with our beloved companion, for she really didn't seem any worse than a bit slow when out on her morning walks. It was almost as if Jasmine had a sense that she wouldn't be coming back and wanted to make the most of her visit there one final time, summoning strength and energy from the very depths of her being. Then, immediately we returned home following this trip, we were given the upsetting news that she had a malignant melanoma in her eye and under the guidance of our vet made the difficult decision to have the tumour and eyeball removed to save her the future agony of a possible catastrophic glaucomatous incident. The operation itself was straight-forward and successful, but the vet did caution us that there was a possibility that the cancer may have spread. But we didn't need or want to know more, we knew we would not allow her to suffer at all. Having any more knowledge would not have helped us in any way to enjoy our remaining time together, it would have brought only worry and sadness into our home.

Then, in December, one Thursday a few weeks after her eye surgery Jasmine stopped eating altogether, something unheard of for her. Her appetite had always been enthusiastic and a solid mark of her wellbeing – not for nothing had we nicknamed her 'the hoover'. Thinking she may have caught a chill – her last walk to the park had been in the snow a day before – we tried everything to entice her to eat, tempting her with morsels of her favourite roast chicken, scrambled egg and braised beef with no success. The vet told us that she had fluid on the lungs and gave her antibiotics, diuretics and an appetite stimulant, saying we should call her if there was any deterioration. By Saturday Jasmine had still eaten nothing at all and spent her time tucked in her bed. We knew this was serious and the vet warned that if there was no improvement by the Monday, it was unlikely that it was the chest infection we had hoped it might be. A lot went unsaid but everything was understood. Sunday, we spent all day cuddling her, trying to encourage her to eat. We prepared all her old favourites but she showed no interest and couldn't bring herself to eat even the tiniest mouthful. That evening, we cuddled closer to each other and later I cried myself to sleep. In the morning we headed to the vet, our hearts heavy and our minds muddled by the sadness of what was happening. One final time Jasmine left her home in our arms, wrapped warm in our love. Once at the surgery, an X-ray confirmed that she had lung tumours and we made the heart-rending decision to say goodbye to our friend. It was, mercifully, a peaceful passing as she slipped away in our arms under the expert and loving care of our vet, Kam, and Jaime, the wonderfully kind nurse who had known her for many of her fourteen and a half years. This was the saddest day of my life and I felt such consuming grief that it was physically painful. However much we had accepted this would happen one day, the reality of the emotional agony of losing Jasmine was hard to bear.

CHAPTER TWO

Reborn

*'I measure every Grief I meet
With narrow, probing, eyes –
I wonder if It weighs like Mine –
Or has an easier size'*

– 'I MEASURE EVERY GRIEF I MEET',
EMILY DICKINSON

Following Jasmine's death, we were both gripped by a terrible unshakeable sadness. Although she had been old and tired, and we had mentally reconciled ourselves to the inescapable facts of life and death long before it occurred, the reality rather than the theory was much harder to manage. Despite her frailty, she had remained the same central character in our family until her very last moments and we felt bereft without her presence. There was a tremendous sense of emptiness in the house and as my work is home-based, my practical inability to escape the hole left by her death compounded a sense of loss and isolation. I was consumed by the most painful of emotions: grief.

Melancholic thoughts had plagued me for weeks before she finally left us as the grim possibility following her eye operation that there might be unknown tumours perniciously eating away at my beautiful old lady affected me daily. It was all too unbearable to cope with unless I had a plan for how we would move on without our constant companion. This in itself brought emotional conflict as I was torn by feelings of guilt and agonies of disloyalty as I watched her decline but planned for life without her. Jasmine had brought us so much happiness that I knew I had to pay tribute to her through bringing a similarly characterful dog into our lives again. This we decided we would do without delay when the day came that she finally left us. Thus it was that shortly after we said goodbye to Jasmine, I set about finding another miniature schnauzer to fill the enormous void she left us with. I know for some people this may have appeared unseemly swift but, for us, it was our way of continuing to love her, to ensure that she would stay amidst us in some form. I could not resign myself to the loss of my friend without knowing she might be close by, even if I could no longer see or touch her. If we found the right dog to bring into our world, I knew I would sense that she was still with me.

If I could have cloned Jasmine I would have, as no other dog seemed suitable to follow in her footsteps – or at least in theory I think I would have, though probably not in all reality. We had loved her so dearly that neither of us could imagine loving a dog that didn't in some way strongly resemble her. Over the years we had grown accustomed to the cheeky, exuberant, clever nature of miniature schnauzers and come to understand that many of Jasmine's most endearing traits weren't accidental: they were highlights, or as some may say, challenges of the schnauzer breed. This time around, though I knew a lot more about the ins and outs of sourcing a puppy and I was determined to choose wisely. The guilt of my first foray into puppy buying had been sharpened over the years as I became more aware of what commercial puppy breeding can entail.

But with this determination to get the right puppy from a good background came breeder waiting lists and the uncertainty of not knowing exactly when and if a litter of puppies was going to be available. Reputable breeders of purebred dogs are highly sought after and it is common that they will have people eagerly awaiting a litter. In fact many will not contemplate breeding without ensuring a waiting list of homes for the puppies is already in place. It can take many months for a buyer to have their puppy confirmed by a breeder. All this, whilst very laudable in terms of ensuring compatibility between buyer, breeder and puppy, is not in the least convenient when wanting to bring home a puppy as soon as possible. This inconvenience undoubtedly gets exploited by commercial-scale breeders and puppy farmers who produce a never-ending supply of puppies with few scruples. Patience when choosing a lifetime companion is most certainly a virtue and always to be encouraged; convenience of the buyer should never be placed above good breeding practices. However, circumstances are always individual and in our case a dog to heal a couple of broken hearts was needed. My grief was piercingly deep and I knew that it would only begin to soften once we found our new companion. I had my eyes wide open and wouldn't be burying any misgivings I felt about any breeders I might come across. Instead I began a thorough nationwide search to find a breeder with puppies available in the near future, knowing it might take me longer than ideal, but I put my mind to it and hoped for the best.

We were keen to give a home to a rescue dog, and in Jasmine's later years often regretted not adopting a second dog when she was young and active enough to enjoy having a new friend. As she moved into her last years we had left it too late but the hours of research I spent looking into the world of rescue and adoptions revealed that unlike some breeds, schnauzers don't come up so often in shelters. Good news for schnauzers, but it meant a fair degree of patience was needed on our part for it would be a question of waiting for a suitable one to come along. This presented us with a dilemma: seeing as we were set on having a miniature schnauzer, by only considering adoption this meant that we could be waiting for months and months without a dog in our home. This I found impossible to accept for I could not reconcile myself with Jasmine's passing so we decided to forge on with finding the perfect puppy, and in addition to this we would adopt one when a suitable companion came up for rehoming. We had a plan that didn't involve learning to be patient and I had a major distraction from my grief.

As I had set no geographical limits on my search, in theory this meant that I would have a lot of breeders to work through. However, I knew that buying a puppy to my convenient time scale meant that I needed to be extra vigilant if I was to avoid the unscrupulous or badly bred puppies that might be advertised. I was acutely sensitive to the tricky timing as around Christmas and New Year is prime time for puppy farmers to make their money with people buying pets as presents and then dumping them in rescue shelters when the holiday novelty wears off. Whilst I wanted to do nothing that would inadvertently contribute to this annually growing problem, I recognised that even buying a puppy with shelters overflowing with perfectly healthy dogs would be doing this. Reputable breeders are wary of breeding litters for availability at Christmas and the few that might have litters would in all likelihood be going to homes that had long been reserved. As well as looking for a puppy I looked too at rescue organisations on the off chance I might find a schnauzer looking for a home, but had little hope this would be successful in the immediate future.

Looking into the minefield that breeding is, my first priority was to ensure the relevant parental health checks had been done before mating, and those for the puppies, and the breeder fully embraced this, didn't skirt round any issues or give me any half-baked reasons as to why they hadn't done it. In the process I came across a few who were so slippery on the subject that I found it all very depressing. As far as looks of the puppies was concerned, I know that Jasmine would not have met the breed standard for miniatures – she was a few inches too tall for a start and had one wonky sticking-up ear giving her a charmingly endearing look, but one which would have failed miserably to impress in the show ring. The show world doesn't interest us. What we love is the personality of schnauzers and it wouldn't matter in the least if our puppy grew too tall, or her coat was too soft to meet the official breed standard. In my search, the more important criteria was that the breeder was devoted to breeding healthy dogs with a beautiful temperament, that the dogs lived within the home and the breeder undertook the requisite health screening of both parents and puppies. It is a serious concern in some breeds that in evolutionary terms, major changes have occurred extremely quickly and genetic diversity is so small, with only a handful of prize-winning dogs being used to father the majority of puppies that major health problems are present, or developing. Small gene pools are never going to be a good idea for any species. Fortunately, miniature schnauzers are one of the breeds with relatively low levels of problems arising from breeding primarily for appearance. Good breeders concentrate on producing healthy puppies in terms of both personality and the physical characteristics of the breed in question and I hoped my extensive search would result in a puppy meeting all criteria, but after the health checks and screening, the breeding home environment is what mattered most to me. Commercial priorities also had to be non-apparent and my senses were already primed to detect anything that looked like a puppy dealer.

I also knew that blindly trusting the breeding practices of some of those in the world of dog showing would be no guarantee that the parent dogs lived in ways I would consider the best for any dog. In the course of researching for this book, I have had stories shared with me of dogs from breeders with solid reputations in the show world, but whose discarded breeding stock display similar disturbing behavioural issues to those dogs living in the more overtly concerning end of dog breeding, in the larger-scale facilities such as puppy farms. In the busy end of commercial dog breeding the stud dogs and breeding bitches need to go somewhere when their productive years are over and they don't all live out their retirement years with those for whom they have produced puppies and made money. Many will be found good family homes but others are not so fortunate. In some cases when their lives have been largely confined to producing puppies for what many consider respectable breeders, they can still be left psychologically traumatised and struggle to adjust to new lives in the home, having lived in kennels all their lives.

Although the pain of losing Jasmine remained acute, my grief did focus me in my search for our new friend and eventually, after many phone calls and emails, lots of dead ends and contact with a fair amount of breeders screaming out to be avoided, I found what I was looking for. The breeder was a three hundred-mile round trip away and we brought home our delightful new puppy on a cold and snowy day in January 2011. When we had first visited the breeder, there were two available puppies from a litter of eight. The experience was so different to when I chose Jasmine many years before. On entering the home, we were introduced to the mother of the puppies without needing to ask and she seemed such a calm and gentle soul as she came and investigated us both. As she nuzzled into our hands, checking us out and who knows, perhaps searching for flaws in those who were about to take one of her babies, we were left in no doubt that she must have produced a seductive litter of pups. We were not disappointed as we met the whole bunch of wriggling, plump puppies all playfully tumbling over each other in their playpen in the family's dining room. There was a choice of two: one beautifully dark-coloured girl and one lighter, closer in colouring to Jasmine and we were both instantly reminded of her. I favoured the darker girl, thinking her colouring was stunning, but Michel immediately fell in love with the other one, who was cuddling into his neck with no hint of reserve – that was it, she was the one! Once the hard and time-consuming task of finding the right breeder was done, for us choosing from her litter was as simple as an endearing puppy cuddle. The decision was swift and final and not once has either of us regretted it.

During the two weeks we had to wait before we could bring her home, the mood in our house lifted as puppy preparations took off. Shopping for essentials brought back many once forgotten fun memories of Jasmine's first days with us. We were able to reminisce with warm smiles instead of tears as we chatted to people about our new puppy as Jasmine's puppyhood and youth came alive in our minds once again. I felt deep gratitude for being able to share her life and joys even though it ended with such sorrow. She was with us every moment of each day as we prepared for this new phase in our lives. I felt her presence the whole time and as happy reminders of her long and carefree life came to me, the raw pain of my grief was gently soothed. The words of the Persian poet Rumi, on a card sent by a friend when she heard of Jasmine's death, rang deep and true,

Don't grieve. Anything you lose comes round in another form

and I so felt that this was the case with our puppy. Naming her was a matter to which I gave a lot of thought and something I found surprisingly difficult. A name is not just a tag by which I call my pets – I'm fascinated by names and enjoy knowing their origins, meanings behind them and the reasons why people choose what they do, whether for their children or pets. For me there is meaning in all names and it was a process that had been churning over in my mind for many months. For the last year or so of Jasmine's life when thoughts of losing her became all too frequent I had long pondered guiltily on what we might name her successor. I had always thought that I would stick to a floral theme for our pets, with Rosie the cat in our home it seemed appropriate and top contenders for whoever followed in Jasmine's steps were Lily and Iris. However, once the time came and we had actually lost her, my previous enthusiasm for floral names quickly faded and sticking to a theme for me seemed too abstract and detached a way to choose our puppy's name. With Jasmine's passing, I felt choked with guilt whenever I thought about the names I had previously conjured. Tangled up in my grief were regretful thoughts of how I could ever have been thinking about naming a puppy whilst Jasmine had been very much alive and still with us.

But, once we had found our puppy, a name needed choosing and so I set about deciding on one that would be suitably special for the dog that followed in Jasmine's companionable footsteps. By chance I happened across the French name Renée and liked the sweet musicality of its pronunciation. More than this, the meaning sealed my decision as soon as I discovered it: the traditional meaning and translation of Renée is 'reborn'. There couldn't be a finer, more perfect name for the dog in whom the spirit of Jasmine would live on; she wasn't lost to us, she was still with us in another form and our puppy's name embodied this sense. When I told a few friends and family members and spelt it to them, enough people anglicised the pronunciation to a harsher, less beautiful version to my ears – 'Reeeneee' – that I decided to adapt the spelling and opted for Renae. After all, she'd never care how it was spelt. Our cute little puppy could now go happily through life with a name that held the essence of our endless love for Jasmine.

Having made many mistakes with Jasmine's training and us learning a lot more over the years about how to be good dog owners and to be able to fulfil a dog's needs, we were keen that Renae would have every opportunity to develop into the perfect dog, or as close as could be. Also we knew much more about the character of miniature schnauzers and were determined to bring out the best in Renae and to minimise any less desirable traits such as the vocal reactivity that Jasmine had so tenaciously displayed. We were still intent on adopting a schnauzer and this gave us extra motivation to work hard with Renae's training to ensure that she would shape up to be the perfect companion for any dog we might eventually bring into our lives that may have issues.

Renae's training began as soon as she joined our home and we worked consistently and with a clear focus towards enabling her to develop into the brilliant dog we knew she could be. From the beginning we devoted time and attention to getting things right. In preparation for her arrival, I had done many hours of reading and research into modern methods of training and for some while had pursued a growing amateur interest in dog psychology. We both felt pretty well equipped and knowledgeable enough to cope with adopting a dog that may require an experienced home. At that stage, we never anticipated that the dog who would eventually join us would be as traumatised and damaged and have as many issues as poor Susie-Belle did.

CHAPTER THREE

Spotting
Susie-Belle

'Life is a series of natural and spontaneous changes. Don't resist them – that only creates sorrow. Let reality be reality. Let things flow naturally forward in whatever way they like'
— LAO TZU

Whilst enjoying life with Renae and relishing the task of steering her through puppyhood and into exuberant adolescence I regularly scoured the internet animal rescue sites. I knew I had to be patient not least so that Renae had time to enjoy her puppyhood free from the challenges of introducing another dog. We loved having a puppy in the house again and good memories surfaced of many amusing antics Jasmine went through that with all the concerns of old age in her last years we'd forgotten about. Having so recently lost our special friend, we were determined to enjoy every single moment of Renae's life with her and not to rush her through any of it. Whilst she had helped fill the gaping void left by Jasmine, she was very much her own dog and we wanted to make sure that she had every opportunity to enjoy life to the full. Although intent on one day adopting a dog, I gave myself a regular talking to, to remind myself that the time was not yet right to bring in another dog, however much I wanted it to happen. Patience has never been my strength and whilst I recognised in my head that Renae had to reach a suitable stage of maturity for any adoption to stand the best chance of success, my heart yearned to help a dog in need and I was sure that we would be a two-dog family before the year was out.

It wasn't long before my interest was caught by a rescue organisation that took in ex-puppy farm breeding dogs to find them homes in which they could safely live out the remainder of their days. As I investigated further it appeared that miniature schnauzers were unfortunately a popular target for the puppy farmers and this particular organisation seemed to have a steady number on their hands. The schnauzer's small, neat size, reputed low allergenic non-moulting coats and the ridiculous growing popularity of expensive, so-called designer crossbreed dogs such as schnoodles and schnugs made them a lucrative business for the unscrupulous to exploit. As I trawled through the organisation's web pages the more I read and saw of the shocking state that some of the rescued animals were in, the angrier I felt. How humans could abuse, neglect and discard dogs in this way, and for financial gain, deeply disturbed me and I burned with the injustice I felt on behalf of the poor creatures. But I did not want to feel angry and helpless. Instead, the sense of fury I felt provoked a challenge within me and I was gripped by a determination that we had to offer a home to one of these poor souls. It would be a fitting way for Jasmine's spirit and memory to flourish with Renae as her successor as she was shaping up to be a great dog and I was certain she too could help to heal a damaged and sensitive dog for whom life had been unspeakably cruel.

I couldn't leave the rescue's website for more than a day or so without checking back to scan the pages of photographs of puppy farm survivors. Picture after picture of dogs in terribly traumatised states, poor health and terrified of human contact held my attention. I couldn't bear to read about them and not believe that one day soon we would do something for one of the dogs. As well as schnauzers there were countless other breeds, testament to the current fashions: shih tzus, beagles, bichon frises, poodles, schnoodles, pugs, Labradors, spaniels and others littered the site. One thing they all seemed to have in common was that they were badly scared of humans. People had not been kind to these poor dogs and the natural affinity shared between our species that has developed over millennia had been shattered by those with whom they had had the misfortune to be in contact. The eyes of the dogs in the pictures all told a similar story – they were petrified. I could only imagine what these animals had endured at the hands of those human beings that they had been saved from to leave them in such a recognisably universal state of fear.

By April of that year I had spotted a sad-looking soul who was being fostered in Berkshire. I cannot properly explain what drew me to this particular female, given the curiously exotic name of 'Niramasu' by the shelter. Of all the sad and needy-looking schnauzers that I'd seen, fanciful as it sounds she seemed to call out to me to pay her attention. As soon as I looked into her eyes in the photo I felt an inexplicable connection and hoped that she would be the one to join our family. But April was too early to bring a traumatised dog into our lives or indeed any dog. Renae was only just settling into good solid routines of behaviour and even though I was impatient to get our canine family together, the burden of common sense told me that we needed to wait a while. I knew that if we brought in a dog that required the kind of help an ex-breeding dog would need, one who had never lived in a home nor known normal, healthy human interaction, had everything to learn about living with people, it would be unfair on Renae. She was still a youngster herself and it would be like handing a teenager the responsibility of helping to bring up a new baby. It wouldn't work, or even if we made it work, it wouldn't be the kindest thing to do for either dog. Much as we longed for a two-dog family, and deep as my wish was to do something for a puppy farm survivor, Renae's happiness and wellbeing remained our top priority. For once, I recognised the need to be patient.

Nevertheless, I couldn't shake thoughts of the little dog in Berkshire from my mind. A profound emotional connection had taken root, albeit one-sided at this stage. I soon made the decision to contact her fosterer, Janet, to inquire further. If nothing else, it would be good for me to know more about the reality of bringing a battery farm breeding bitch into our home because reading up on it and thinking we knew enough about it to go ahead was one thing, living with the decision quite another. I felt oddly nervous as I drafted an email to Janet – it seemed so important to me that I came over as someone genuinely capable of being considered an adopter for one of these special dogs, if not Niramasu, another in the future. My heart was now fully set on bringing one of them into our family and my logical mind was rapidly trying to catch up as I worked out what needed to be done to make it happen. I tried to contain my enthusiasm and present myself as a normal, sensible potential adopter rather than the fixated obsessive I felt I was at risk of sounding in my email. Janet quickly replied and we arranged for me to phone the next day. Although it was to be just an informal chat and nothing was intended to come of it with regard to immediately adopting a dog, I wanted to make a decent impression. I was keen not to show an undue level of ignorance of the true extent of what a traumatised dog is like to live with but I knew that I needed to hear the truth too. I considered stretching the truth about Renae's young age, knowing this was likely to be a problem, but thankfully came to my senses before making that mistake. Instead I reminded myself again and again that it was unlikely Niramasu would be coming to live with us, I was just fact-finding for the future and doing my research.

For the rest of that day, I set about reading as much as I could find online about how the dirty business of puppy farming leaves dogs that survive and get to live in homes for the first time in their lives. Some of what I read scared me as the difficulties can be deep and long term. It wasn't the thought of having a dog that had never been house trained, or walked on a lead, or didn't enjoy being handled that seemed hard as I hoped all of this might be overcome with patience and time. No, it was much more the severe psychological trauma these dogs suffer caused by years of living in confinement and experiencing abuse and neglect on a scale that I hated to imagine. Neither Michel nor I had any experience of living with psychologically challenging dogs. I recognised that being well read on a topic doesn't an expert make and knew the reality could be a staggering shock. I hadn't forgotten that the challenges Jasmine had presented us were all of the mundane, routine, normal behavioural type that occur when owners don't know what they're up to and that we hadn't done a very good job of curbing some of her livelier excesses. On the other hand, we seemed to be doing a better job with Renae and I took some comfort in successfully nurturing her beautiful personality. But many times that day I asked myself if a puppy farm survivor was really something we could cope with and what effect this would have on our delightful Renae, whose life was innocent and full of fun without responsibility.

Michel's view was that if I thought we could manage it, he would support me in the decision. He wanted only to do what was right for Renae and left me to pursue and understand the issues in detail, knowing that I would do my homework and take seriously the responsibility for any decision we made. As I read more about the lives of puppy farm rescues, people's stories were on one hand heartening as they shared progress reports and I saw pictures of adopted dogs eventually living healthy, normal lives but on the other, the scale of what we might be taking on seemed almost overwhelming. Multiple health concerns, behavioural issues which could not always be successfully worked through and a requirement for lots and lots of patience seemed to be common themes. Following stories online that day and into the evening confirmed for me that we would be entering new territory; it would be a big challenge and require a level of commitment that we should not take lightly.

Early the next day I called Janet. But I needn't have worried about her vetting me over the phone for as soon as we spoke we got along well and by the end of the conversation, I knew that whatever she advised, I would be guided by. If she detected any hint of my growing obsession, it didn't put her off, nor did she let on. Janet had fostered ex-breeding dogs for a number of years, as well as being a manager for an independent animal rescue centre. She very clearly knew what she was doing and I respected that. I explained our circumstances and expressed my wish to adopt an ex-puppy farm breeder but before I could stop myself, my enthusiasm got the better of me and I asked about meeting Niramasu, who Janet affectionately called Susie. Janet gently reined in my eagerness and explained that Renae was too young to be able to cope with bringing a dog like Susie into her life. I slumped into my chair, deflated, as although this was something I knew in my heart, to have it said aloud to me was disappointing.

Janet continued to talk at the end of the phone and I did my best to concentrate as she talked me through the work – and patience – that would be involved in adopting a dog like Susie, not that she would be the one for me as Renae was too young. Yes, I got that point. I knew the reality before it had been said, although Janet of course needed to say it. But knowing it didn't stop me from feeling that Susie had been wrenched away at the embryonic stage of starting life with us. It had all been in my head, though. From seeing her photograph I had sped through our imaginary early days together – already she was running happily with Renae in the park before I'd picked up the phone that morning. I was stupid and impatient and not in the least bit sensible about the whole matter and I'd come crashing down the moment Janet had quietly, patiently, told me the sobering facts of life as far as Susie and I were concerned. As I gathered myself together, I focussed again on Janet's words, explaining that the dogs she fostered had never known a normal life, never lived with anything other than harsh treatment – they only related to humans with terror and avoidance and had everything to learn about living in a home. Hearing this directly from someone who had fostered so many of these dogs brought me to my senses and slammed home the reality of what I had spent hours and hours reading. This would be serious, hard work. Though nothing like raising a puppy – a puppy is a clean slate – this would be a dog with major baggage. Renae was just a baby and needed and deserved all our attention. I knew I had to force myself to forget about Susie and wait until Renae had sufficiently matured – by which time Susie would undoubtedly have been adopted into another home.

Maybe sensing my barely disguised disappointment Janet went on to say that she had quite a regular intake of foster schnauzers. She had long loved the breed, had two of her own minis, as well as four other dogs, and assured me that even though the timing wasn't right for Susie to join us, there would certainly be another come along at some point in the future. At this I perked up but then quickly sobered as I realised that whilst this was good news on one level, the irony was that it also meant that the suffering in the puppy farms is endless for these dogs. A steady supply of foster schnauzers might satisfy my desire to bring one eventually into our loving and safe home, but that meant there was also a steady supply of poor wretches suffering in the commercial dog breeding industry. Janet and I agreed that we would stay in touch through the year and I asked that she should let me know how Susie got on in her new home when one came along.

Meanwhile we continued to work with Renae and continue her training and to fully enjoy our time with her. She was such a lively, intelligent pup that she picked things up quickly and our bond with her became closer and closer. It was a complete pleasure to see how she was maturing into the fantastic friend we hoped she would one day prove to be for whichever special dog joined her. As she thrived, plans for our upcoming long summer trip to France took shape. Holidays there were such a regular feature of our lives that it was important that car travel was not a problem for Renae. From day one we had been getting her used to lots of trips and she was at ease travelling with us for both long and short car journeys. For many of her 14 years, Jasmine had travelled with us over the Channel every few weeks but the summer trip would be Renae's first visit abroad as we had to wait the requisite six months for her pet passport to be valid. We were both itching to take her out to our house in southwest France as we knew that she would love the space, freedom and the excitement of her first foreign holiday. It's so solidly a home from home for us and our time spent there forms such a large part of our lives that we wanted to share it with her as soon as we could.

The six-week long summer trip had been on my mind all year as it presented another barrier to adopting a dog. I couldn't possibly do it before we went to France as the dog wouldn't have its passport or be ready to travel and there was no way we would leave it behind with others or in kennels. Once Susie had burrowed into my heart and mind, this presented another hurdle to her adoption for I knew that even if I had been able to persuade Janet that Renae was old enough, Susie couldn't come to France in the summer. Yet another reason I had to stop thinking about her. But try as I might, I couldn't stop myself taking a look at her photo online and scanning regularly to see what updates, if any, there were on her. I fantasised on how I could somehow reserve her for the next few months so that we could get the summer trip out of the way: Renae would be older and we could apply to adopt this little schnauzer who had so thoroughly stolen my heart. Common sense told me that there was no way that she would, or should be reserved for us – the priority for Janet and the rescue organisation was to find the right permanent home as quickly as possible. Janet had not hidden that from me but still I struggled to let Susie go from my mind.

I knew that it wasn't ethical for me to be thinking of my own wishes, however much I believed Susie would fit right in with us. The anger I felt towards the people who had caused her to suffer was focussed on me giving her the good life I knew we could. One of my favourite writers, Maya Angelou, wrote that,

> *Bitterness is like cancer. It eats upon the host. But anger is like fire. It burns it all clean.*

This was what I wanted to do for Susie – to take away all that had been bad for her and burn it, to make her world right, give her the life she should have. On the other hand, I knew that she was in a very good temporary foster home with Janet and if only she could stay there for a few more weeks, she might still be available to join us after the summer. There was a glimmer of hope that this may prove to be the case as she did have some health concerns that any potential adopter would have to take responsibility for and this might deter some people from applying for her. I hung onto that, feeling bad that Susie's poor health gave me cause for hope and contacted Janet again to ask if I could come and visit for the day. I didn't say much about wanting to meet Susie specifically, although I'm sure that Janet saw through my feigned casualness as I suggested bringing Renae just to see how she got along with all the schnauzers that Janet had around.

As well as her foster work, many of Janet's colleagues and friends at her rescue centre also had ex-puppy farm schnauzers that they themselves had adopted who regularly spent the day at the Centre. For us it would be schnauzer heaven for the day and a good test for Renae to see how well she got along with the other dogs. Janet agreed without hesitation, the date was set and I tried to stop fretting about whether an adopter might come along in the meantime and apply for Susie.

CHAPTER FOUR

Amongst the Misfits

'Can you understand? Someone, somewhere, can you understand me a little, love me a little? For all my despair, for all my ideals, for all that – I love life. But it is hard, and I have so much – so very much to learn'
– THE JOURNALS OF SYLVIA PLATH, *SYLVIA PLATH*

The Diana Brimblecombe Animal Rescue Centre is an independent animal shelter founded over forty years ago and now located on a fourteen-acre site deep in the Berkshire countryside. On the morning of my first visit I unintentionally explored a lot of that countryside as I tried to find the Centre and eventually, ninety minutes late, I arrived having got hopelessly lost. Not one to take being late lightly, I had been stressing in the car about what kind of first impression I was going to create. If I couldn't arrive on time, could I ever be trusted to adopt one of Janet's foster schnauzers, let alone the special Susie? My ridiculous anxieties were completely misplaced for Janet and her team at DBARC could not have been more welcoming or kinder to the frazzled, frantic woman turning up late for a meeting with their schnauzers. Most of the dogs I was about to meet had been adopted by Janet, her staff and volunteers, but she did have some that were also being fostered by herself and her friend Donna, as well as the one I had really come to meet: Susie.

It was a beautiful sunny day and once I had calmed and collected myself and introduced Janet to Renae (who had been given a pep talk on the way there about first impressions being all-important), we went along to an enormous grassy outside area where I was greeted with one of the most delightful scenes I'd ever witnessed. There appeared to be schnauzers everywhere and when they spotted their visitors they simultaneously broke out into an excitable, vocal schnauzer welcome. It was utterly adorable and I felt honoured to be treated to such a warm and noisy schnauzery greeting. Never had I seen – or heard – so many schnauzers in one place. There must have been around twenty, all barking their hearts out and welcoming us into their space. Renae entered the schnauzer zone calmly and with admirable confidence. She didn't seem at all fazed by the frenzy and I felt a sense of pride at her sociability and good doggy manners. Relief was also secretly flooding through me as she had successfully passed her first initiation into one day sharing her life with another dog. Our dedication to ensuring that she was well socialised from the word go was clearly paying off.

Although a visit to any dog show gives an opportunity to see lots of similar looking dogs in the various classes together, at that stage I had never done that, nor was this like a dog show as this was a genuinely unique experience. Although I was standing amongst a group of miniature schnauzers – the noise alone told me that – this was no perfectly shaped, sized, coiffed and immaculate group of privileged, top-notch schnauzers that a show experience would yield. Best described as a bunch of noisy misfits, they were in a class all their own – the most special and demanding class of all. These were puppy farm survivors with tales to tell, if only we knew. There was Marty, the three-legged gentleman, happily hopping around making friends with Renae. On arrival as a foster dog with Donna his leg was so deformed and useless the decision was made that the kindest thing for him would be to remove it and he hasn't looked back. He now lives happily as Donna's adopted tripawd (three-legged dog).

Then there was Harley – a petite young thing, looking so small and delicate but with the most remarkable upright ears that seemed almost as big as her body. I later found out that she had been fostered as a very sickly young pup, having been discarded by the puppy farmer and saved from destruction by kind rescuers. As Janet nursed her through her first few weeks, she was diagnosed with a serious heart condition that in all likelihood would shorten her life. Finding the right environment where her health needs would be taken care of was essential; she was adopted into the safe and loving home of Julie, a member of Janet's staff. Laurie too was being fostered – a tiny, beautiful black female, blinded in one eye at some stage in the puppy farm with what Janet's vet thought must have been an untreated penetrating eye injury. Awful to imagine what suffering she had endured, but to see her that day, bouncing around playfully with Renae, was testament to the resilience of these amazing survivors. Like the beautiful Dolly, a young, lively female with coordination problems that most likely had an as yet undiagnosed neurological basis. She was later adopted by Donna and will eventually receive whatever specialist veterinary care her condition requires, should it deteriorate in the future.

At that stage when I visited, Janet had two of her own schnauzers, three collies and one Japanese Spitz. Her schnauzers, Monkey and Munchkin, had both arrived with her as puppy farm rejects. Munchkin was Janet's first schnauzer adoptee and her first foray into the world of ex-breeders, having lost her beloved miniature schnauzer Cinders after fourteen years together. Soon after, Monkey arrived as a very young puppy to be fostered, sold with her sister to a dealer whose groomer couldn't get near them both – they were so snappy from fear. He called the local rescue and said that if they wouldn't take them he would have no option but to take them back to the place where he'd got them, who would dispose of them by shooting since they were commercially worthless. Thankfully the rescue then made contact with Janet and the sisters duly arrived with her. Just four months old, they were very scared and fear-aggressive, the undoubted result of severe abuse during their short lives. Monkey's less aggressive and braver sister was soon rehomed, but it took Janet several months before she was able to safely touch Monkey without being bitten. Janet adopted her but even in her expert care, she has stayed very wary of people, and will bark fiercely at anyone she is unsure about. On the day I first met her, she was the noisiest schnauzer by far and this after four years of constant work, plenty of socialisation and handling. She is a permanent work in progress, but clearly much loved by Janet.

As I sat and savoured the marvellous sight of so many dogs in one place being entirely at ease with one another despite their individual special needs and backgrounds, with Renae settling happily amongst them, I wondered at the beauty of the dogs that allowed themselves, despite the suffering they had endured at the hands of humans, to move onwards to enjoy new lives. I was struck that they were now contentedly living out lives that many dogs, Renae included, took for granted. All my reading and research up to that point had provided the theory, but here I was amidst the reality: for those who survive the battery farming of dogs the injuries, the suffering, the psychological, behavioural and ongoing health issues were all there in a small and special corner of Berkshire for me to witness. When Mark Twain wrote,

> *I have been studying the traits and dispositions of the "lower animals" (so called) and contrasting them with the traits and dispositions of man. I find the result humiliating to me.*

He couldn't have envisioned the massive scale of animal suffering that the modern commercial breeding of dogs now entails. How he would write of matters had he lived today we can only imagine.

After a short while of watching Renae play with the boisterous younger dogs, happily wrestling and rough and tumbling with them, we moved to a quieter part of the play area where a few of the older, calmer schnauzers had settled, having done their meet and greet and checking us out. Here, for the first time I saw Susie. Of course Janet already knew she was the real reason for my visit that day and with a warm smile introduced me to the little dog who didn't yet know how much she had stolen my heart. Although my instinct was to rush excitedly over, pick up this gentle creature and wrap her in the biggest embrace she had ever experienced, thankfully I managed to contain myself and not terrorise Susie with my exuberance. Instead I took a deep breath and calmly moved closer to her as she pottered peacefully around paying scant attention to the excitable playing of the younger dogs nearby. She was much smaller than I had imagined, very skinny and her thin, patchy coat was a mottled mixture of brown patches amongst the pepper-and-salt schnauzer coat. Janet explained that where the brown patches were, this was newly grown coat – when she had arrived she had been almost bald, with only a few tufts of filthy fluff here and there. The extent of brown remained evidence of the shocking hair loss she had suffered through a terrible combination of years of accumulated filth, skin infection, infestation, hormonal disruption and neglect. It is not uncommon to find totally bald breeding bitches in puppy farms caused by poor nutrition coupled with high lactation demands and repeated pregnancies.

As I crouched down near Susie, just managing to restrain myself from getting too close for fear of frightening her, after a few seconds she looked across at me and to my huge delight came trotting over, stopping just out of reach but definitely curious about the odd stranger who seemed utterly fascinated by her. Before either of us had time to move closer, Renae, seeing me crouch, came bounding over to see what was happening and the first meeting between Susie and Renae took place. Noses touched, sniffs were exchanged and all went better than I could have hoped for as these two females, living such different lives, went about their canine greetings as naturally as dogs do.

Looking at Renae next to Susie, I was struck by how pampered and privileged Renae seemed. For a start she appeared enormous – she was still holding onto her puppy plumpness and stood a little taller than Susie. Her coat was thick, soft and shiny and she oozed confidence as she moved off to look for some more fun, having reassured herself that she wasn't missing out on anything in our quiet corner. She was in her element amidst all the schnauzers. I was delighted with her but reflected that as she had never had any reason to worry about anything in her life thus far, why would she not enjoy a day out meeting a whole gang of potential new friends? Why would this not be just the most fun for a happy, healthy young pup? She was not a dog who had to work through any anxieties or fear of humans for she had mercifully never had cause to form them. Whilst I was of course pleased to see her doing so well, it also served to bring home to me just how sad the lives of Susie and all the other puppy farm survivors I met that day had once been. Their bravery in overcoming their poor beginnings and in many cases years of difficulties hit me full force.

Eventually I dragged Renae and myself away from the dogs and we moved to Janet's office. I wanted to know more about Susie and to sound out Janet as to what she thought about the timing for one day bringing home one of her foster dogs now that she had met us. I knew that I would have to wait for her to consider Renae mature enough to be the good sister she would have to be. On the basis of her sterling performance with the dogs that day, I was hopeful that it wouldn't be too long a wait. Janet told me that whilst Susie was doing well and her health continued to improve, she did have cataracts in both eyes and would most likely one day go blind. This would deter many people from applying to adopt her and those who did would have to be very clear about what her future might be if her cataracts were left untreated. Although the news of her likely blindness was a shock, this did not deter me from wanting to be considered as her adopter if she was still with

Janet after our summer holiday. Living with a blind dog didn't worry me – I knew we could adapt and make sure that she had all she needed to be happy and fulfilled. If anything, hearing the terrible news about Susie's eyes brought me closer to her as it reminded me of nursing Jasmine through her eye operation and I knew that I wouldn't be fazed in dealing with any similar issues. How Susie would cope with the loss of her sight was of course something none of us could know.

Janet had found homes for blind puppy farm fosters over the years and they had got along fine in their new homes but their families needed to make suitable arrangements for this to happen. One such puppy was ten-week-old Mouse, born blind and discarded by her commercial breeder as worthless before being thankfully fostered by Janet. Mouse may not have left the puppy factory she came into the world in with the same kind of issues caused over years that an ex-breeder or stud dog does, but she was nevertheless a victim of bad commercial breeding. Had she not had the good fortune to be taken into rescue and found a loving, safe home, there is no doubt she would have met a swift and brutal end. It is horrible to imagine what does happen to all the many puppies born with obvious afflictions in these places as most certainly never make their way to safety. I left Janet that day more determined than ever that Susie would one day come home to us.

CHAPTER FIVE

Susie-Belle's
First Day Out

'Yesterday is gone. Tomorrow has not yet come. We have only today. Let us begin'

– MOTHER THERESA

Shortly after our visit, Janet called to let me know that she had visited Susie's veterinary ophthalmologist and it had been agreed to operate on her left eye to remove the cataract and give her a new artificial lens. This was very good news indeed as first and foremost, assuming the surgery was a success, Susie's sight would be completely restored in that eye. Even should the cataract in her other eye cause problems at some point in the future, she would not be blind. But, in addition to me being delighted that Janet had arranged for this expensive, specialist, sight-saving surgery, I was secretly pleased as this also meant Susie would not be available for adoption for several weeks as she recovered from the operation. I quickly calculated that given the estimated recovery time, this would bring us very close to the end of August and by then we would be home from France. Renae would also be that bit more mature and surely we would be in with a very good chance of being able to offer Susie a new home at the end of the summer. I was excited – it seemed that far from our trip to France being a barrier to adopting Susie, being away would provide an ideal distraction from what, if my plans succeeded, would be a long wait to bring home Renae's new sister.

At this stage Janet and I were in regular contact. I was eager to hear how all her dogs were getting along but none more than Susie. She now had a new foster-buddy, Patti – a terrified, timid schnauzer, who had arrived completely blinded by cataracts in both eyes. Miniature schnauzers are one of the breeds affected by congenital and hereditary cataracts. Because it is a recognised problem, responsible breeders will ensure any dogs used for breeding and their puppies are eye tested. No dogs that fail the testing should ever be bred from, but of course unscrupulous parts of the puppy breeding industry do not concern itself with such details. Cataracts can be both hereditary and congenital, occur with age, from certain health issues and are almost certainly linked to poor nutrition. If Susie's or Patti's (or any of the other dogs with cataracts that Janet had taken in) were hereditary or congenital cataracts, their puppies would be likely to develop them.

Over the years Janet had seen an alarming number of dogs affected by cataracts come from the puppy farms and she is only one of thousands of fosterers of ex-puppy farm dogs of all breeds around the country. The number of dogs potentially affected presents a frightening prospect. Without the correct veterinary care, the affected dogs will go blind and without the right homes and families to offer support to these dogs, their lives are severely affected. People buying a puppy and not knowing its origins, not being aware of the need for eye or other health screening in their chosen breed, are potentially sitting on a health time bomb with their pets. Breeding in the worse puppy farms is done with no consideration for the maintenance of healthy breed standards but purely for profit. The reduction or elimination of genetic and hereditary problems almost certainly never passes through the minds of those involved, resulting in the passage of these conditions and diseases through generations. It is a terrible legacy of puppy farming that dogs carrying health problems are bred from and their cute little puppies will eventually suffer the consequences of these shameful practices. If the problems are obvious at the time of potential sale the puppies will be unsaleable and disposed of like any damaged, worthless product. In establishments where there may be a hint of conscience, or a professional commercial front that covers the truth, the puppies will be euthanised by a veterinary practitioner; in the worst places, they will be dealt with the cheap way by the gun.

The weekend before her cataract surgery was scheduled for the Monday, Janet agreed that I could take Susie out for the day. This was a good indicator of her confidence in me as a potential adopter and my excitement rose as the day drew close. From Renae's earliest days with us I had been keen to get her out and about with other dogs as much as we could, both for her socialisation but also to ensure that she would be happy having another dog in her life. Since we'd brought her home at the start of the year, we had joined an online UK-based schnauzer forum and regularly met with other owners around and about the south of England. The forum was a great way to network and arrange meet ups and walks; all the dogs that came along loved them and for a young pup like Renae the walks and events proved to be excellent socialisation. We were always keen to take part in any that we could get to, or arrange ourselves and on this day there was a walk being held close to where we live. This meant that we could get up to Berkshire early in the day to collect Susie from Janet's, head out to the walk and then get her home in time for tea, having enjoyed her first big day out – and the first of many more to come if my hopes and plans came together.

Arriving at Janet's early that morning, it was Michel's first chance to meet the little dog that he had heard so much about and that had taken up so many hours of my attention in recent weeks. Unlike me, he is a naturally relaxed, calm person and where my excitement on our first meeting had been barely containable, Michel's quiet reserve was perfect as Janet brought Susie out to meet us all. He was the ideal balance to my bubbling excitement as we put her in the car with Renae and set off. Janet assured me that she travelled well in the car and so it proved. No sooner had we secured her next to Renae than she settled down to enjoy the ride and gave us no cause for concern on the drive, although this didn't stop me checking from time to time on our very important passenger.

Janet had given me firm instructions not to allow Susie off the lead at all, for whilst she was relatively confident that Susie wouldn't bolt if she became spooked by anything, it was a definite possibility. Some of the foster dogs that Janet cares for cannot be trusted for months on end not to flee at the slightest thing that alarms them. For Janet this is not a problem as she has secure paddocks over several acres in which she can exercise them and get them used to walking on lead, but in the outside world this of course presents a major hazard. But Janet needn't have worried as I had zero intention of letting Susie off-lead; the responsibility weighed heavily on me as we arrived at the car park. Norbury Park lies in the Surrey Hills Area of Outstanding Natural Beauty and is a popular place for dog walkers. It covers an area of around 1,500 acres and has a range of different habitats and wildlife all year round. One of our favourite local walks, it's away from what can be a lot of noise and activity in many other areas in the busy southeast of England where we live. Most of the walking we do there is safe, off-lead and away from any traffic – perfect for a group of excitable dogs to meet up on a Saturday afternoon in early summer.

Already there were a few familiar faces waiting in the car park and the usual schnauzer noise reached a crescendo as more and more dogs arrived ready for the walk. It was a beautiful warm day and the dogs were all getting overexcited, waiting for the walk to start. Michel took responsibility for Renae who was busily meeting friends, old and new, leaving me to concentrate on taking care of Susie amidst all the excitement and high energy. One thing that ex-puppy farm dogs take comfort in is other canine company – they may never have learned to trust humans but usually they feel comfortable around other dogs. That's why organisations that rehabilitate and home dogs from these backgrounds tend to insist they join homes where there is another dog as they learn so much from the resident dog and take comfort in the familiarity of canine company. This after all may have been the only company that a breeding dog had for its entire lifetime before escaping the nightmare of the breeding factory.

As we walked over to join the throng, Susie stayed tucked in behind my feet, head low, body tense but compliant. Some of those coming along to the walk had heard all about Susie via the forum and were keen to meet her, but I knew for her afternoon to go well, it was essential that she wasn't overwhelmed by too much attention. On the other hand, I was determined not to overfuss and to allow her the opportunity to enjoy being out in a new environment. She had a whole lifetime of new walks to look ahead to, this was just the beginning and I did not want to mess it up. Not fussing over Susie was one thing, taking care to ensure she was not getting stressed another – somehow I had to find the right balance if our first day out together was to be a success.

Janet had warned me that she would not like anyone walking behind her – this I later discovered is a very common trait amongst such dogs. In all probability it arises from the many times that they are kicked out of the way, caught in doorways, grabbed by their tails, harshly handled and roughly mated. Nothing good happens to breeding bitches when people are behind them. And so it was that the entire walk, Susie would stop and wait for people to pass her before walking on. She stayed glued to my feet. Whenever she sensed anyone coming up behind us, she would stop still, firmly plant her feet in the ground and not move a muscle until that person had passed. If I tried to encourage her to move forwards, she hunkered down on her haunches, shoulders spread wide, front paws digging into the earth to hang onto the ground. She did not react in this way when it was a dog running up, it was a purely human triggered behaviour but it was 100 per cent ingrained.

That afternoon not a single person walked past Susie without her little body stopping and her terrified eyes staring wide until the perceived danger had passed. Even though Janet had warned me about it, I was still taken aback by this. So much is different when faced with the reality of it happening rather than just hearing or reading about it. Not until I experienced it for myself could I truly understand the impact of what Janet had said. So much hadn't fully registered with me in my obsession to help a puppy farm survivor yet here again, just as at Janet's, where I had seen for the first time the damage done to these dogs, the shocking truth of just what overwhelming fear means for a dog was there for me to witness. This was new territory for someone who until very recently had only had the experience of living and meeting normal, happy, loved, family pets. The terror in Susie's eyes as someone passed her or walked behind her was real and heartwrenching to witness.

Throughout the afternoon's walk Susie was an absolute angel despite her timidity and terror of people coming up from behind. She trotted along perfectly at my heels, not walking a single step ahead of me for that would have been terrifying for her to do. Then, towards the end of the walk, after about an hour or so, she stopped walking. I was at the back of the group as Susie had ensured no one remained behind her and as she sat there on the grass, panting and hot, the rest of the group walked off into the distance. Michel and Renae were nowhere to be seen – in fact I hadn't seen them since the start of the walk as Susie and I dropped to the back. As we stood and looked at each other, I did my best to work out what she needed from me, what I should be doing. I tried to encourage her to continue walking, not wanting to scare or overwhelm her, then I waited and waited for her to carry on. But she wouldn't move a muscle: she just sat there looking at me, speaking to me with her beautiful, scared eyes, but I didn't understand her. I didn't know what she wanted; I was floundering. Should I pick her up and carry her, or would that terrify the life out of her? I tried gently tugging on the lead but she wouldn't budge. Then I tried ignoring her and avoiding eye contact, knowing this can be threatening to dogs. Nothing changed. She wouldn't move. She sat, I stood; we both tried to get the other to understand what was needed.

Then, just as I was deciding that we couldn't stay there much longer but not knowing how we were going to move without me terrifying her, running back along the path came Renae. Sweet, considerate Renae had come to find us. She took one look at the scene and ran straight up to Susie, checking her out. Susie's head came up, her little stump of a tail flicked with recognition, her nose twitched and with Renae trotting slightly ahead, she started to follow her. We were on the move again and once Renae was satisfied that we were following, she gave Susie one final little check as she circled back around her, before hurtling off ahead to once again join the others, who by now had stopped to wait for us to catch up. I silently thanked my gorgeous Renae for helping me out, for saving me from being so hopeless at knowing what Susie needed, for sensing when she was required and for doing exactly what Susie needed her to do. At that moment I knew that Renae was ready to be a sister to Susie.

At the end of the walk, we had drinks at the Bockett's Farm Café, where Susie sat quietly in the shade under the table. I was tired from the emotional excitement as much as from the walk, and if I felt this, I was sure Susie must be exhausted. It had been her first day away from the safety of Janet's familiar surroundings and although we couldn't know for certain how she felt, I was quietly confident that she had at least not hated her day out. She may even have enjoyed herself. I certainly felt that she and Renae had begun to bond and I hoped that she felt some growing connection with me. After our drinks, we said our goodbyes and headed off to Berkshire to drop Susie back at Janet's.

Later, Janet reported that she slept so well that night, no doubt dreaming of her first big day out. It had been a success all round and I was floating on air all that evening whenever I thought about our day. Although she was very timid, Susie had the most trusting, gentle way about her that made me and now Michel fall completely and utterly in love. Even more pleasingly, Renae was so obviously capable of thoughtful attention to Susie that I had no doubts at all that she would one day be a very good sister to our special dog.

CHAPTER SIX

What's in a Name?

'Just because you didn't put a name to something did not mean it wasn't there'
— HANDLE WITH CARE, *JODI PICOULT*

A couple of days after Susie's big day out, she went into the veterinary clinic for her cataract surgery with one of the UK's leading ophthalmologists, Mr Fraser in Oxford. Not all dogs with cataracts can have surgery, or indeed require it, and the surgery is highly specialised. We were incredibly fortunate that Janet arranged for Susie to be evaluated and treated by Mr Fraser, who agreed to do her surgery. The cataract in her left eye was the more serious and was badly affecting her vision so she had it removed and a new artificial lens inserted. Her right eye was at a stage where surgery was not yet indicated and it was decided that with the new lens in her left eye this would most likely be all the surgery she would need as it would

51

preserve her eyesight even if this became a problem in her later years. Once surgery has been performed, cataracts cannot recur, although other problems may arise. The surgery may not have been lifesaving, but by preserving her vision, it was an amazing life-changing procedure for Susie.

On the day of surgery, Susie went along with Patti, the blind fosterer who had recently joined Janet. Patti came out with two new lenses and her eyesight fully restored. From that moment on, her personality underwent a powerful transformation. Unlike the timid, terrified dog that I had seen a couple of days before sitting in Janet's office, cuddled on her knee, she became a different dog. To say she was confident would be stretching it, but during her recovery with Susie, her confidence grew daily. I found it remarkable to wonder what it must be like for a scared blind dog that had known no kindness up until that point in its life to go into surgery and come out being able to see the world around them and be surrounded by love. What an utterly bewildering experience it must be but it would seem that dogs often take it in their stride, live in the moment and begin to enjoy their lives with newly restored vision. This was certainly the case for Patti and she made rapid progress to living a normal life in the weeks she recovered with Susie, back in the safe and loving care on offer at Janet's.

A few weeks later Patti was adopted by a kind family living in the idyllic New Forest in the south of England. She had access to acres and acres of beautiful, open walks right from her doorstep and no doubt with her restored sight, she was able to properly appreciate the beauty that surrounded her. Within months she was a confident dog and within a year or so following her adoption, she was as noisy as any normal miniature schnauzer, living a life free from the fears and darkness that had previously trapped her.

WHAT'S IN A NAME?

When Susie went in for the surgery it had not yet been officially confirmed that we could adopt her but Janet and I had reached an understanding that following her operation I should apply to do so and after the paperwork had been processed and the home-check done, she would be ours. The imminent trip to France that meant we would be out of the country for several weeks was no longer an obstacle for she had to stay with Janet for the duration of her convalescence. I could travel safe in the knowledge that no other potential adopters could sneak in at the last minute and snatch my Susie away to a new home.

With Susie recovering from her surgery, I duly set about completing the paperwork and adoption procedures. The home-check was approved, Janet approved and within days of eye surgery and her first big day out in the world at Norbury Park, that was it: Susie was officially ours. What a life-transforming few days it was for this little dog, who had no idea about what was being planned on her behalf. Now preparations for her coming to her new home at the end of August really took off. Up to the official approval, I had been pretending to be restrained, reminding myself that there was still a chance that we may not be approved as adopters. The only real concern I thought which might have been raised when I submitted the application was Renae's young age but I had talked with Janet at length on this and I trusted that her experienced view would sway it. If she thought Renae was mature enough to be a good sister for Susie, any objections that may be raised by Susie's original rescuers (who had the final say on her new home) would be overcome with Janet's support. In the end, there were no problems: as her fosterer Janet's view was accepted without question that Susie had a safe and appropriate home available to go to with us. Having seen Renae take care of Susie at Norbury Park, I had no worries at all that they would soon be the best of friends.

Once the adoption was officially confirmed, I put my mind to considering a name. I thought long and hard about whether I should change it from Susie – she had after all spent the last few weeks getting used to being called by what was most likely her first ever name. Typically in commercial breeding places, if any identification of the dogs is used, they are given a number. It is not unusual for rescuers, particularly in the worst puppy mills in America, to find dogs with numbered tags tangled into matted fur, or painfully embedded into the poor dog's skin for, as the years pass by, the dogs grow and the original tags become tight around their necks, cutting into the flesh. It is no surprise that commercial breeders fail to name the dogs for, in naming them, they become personal. The depersonalisation of dogs in the battery farming of them simply encourages the abuse; without names it is easier for them to seem not to exist. Naming them would make it a lot harder to view them as mere commodities, livestock to be abused to the point of death – a cash crop with no name.

I believe the naming of our pets is a crucial step in the process of them developing their personality and helps to establish a bond between them and us. Sounds fanciful? Then take a second to ponder a dog called Fang and one named Fifi. Naming our dogs most certainly makes them personal to us and any dog that had so much love awaiting her as Susie did was not to be lightly named. With my penchant for the symbolism of names, I started looking into the origins of the name Susie. When I discovered that Susan derives from the Persian name for lily, a name that I had always thought beautiful and might at one stage have chosen for Renae, it seemed perfect that Susie kept her name. As if that wasn't convincing enough, with the Hebrew root for the name for the lily flower coming from that meaning 'to be joyful, bright or cheerful' it was no longer a question that her name would be kept. Just as Renae was living up to her name with the spirit of Jasmine living on in our house with our adorable pup, so too I hoped that Susie would one day shine bright with joy and happiness. However, whilst I found the name Susie acceptable, it didn't seem quite enough of a name for a dog that I dearly loved even before she had come into my care. Also, it wasn't my choice of name for her – I wanted her name to be something special that I had actively chosen that reflected the already deep emotional connection that I felt with her. It seemed so important that she should have her own special name as a simple but meaningful gift from me.

As I thought about my connection with her, the uniquely precious name I felt she deserved kept slipping away from my consciousness. I knew it was there but somehow I couldn't quite grasp it and bring it to life to adorn her with although I sensed it floating somewhere in my psyche, if only I could find it. For days I dwelt on it. As she would be spending a lot of her time with us in France, a touch of French vogue appealed to me and eventually after many hours of daydreaming and pondering, one morning it appeared in my half-waking thoughts: *belle* the French for beautiful was perfect and my beautiful, brave dog who had survived so much and had so much living to now get on and do became Susie-Belle. This was her name, my gift to her. No one had ever used that name for her before and no one would ever take it from her. It was now the name she would start her new life with. With her ugly past behind her, she could begin afresh, suitably, beautifully named.

We had a short time before heading off to France but before

we went Renae and I made a couple more visits to Janet's to help Susie-Belle get used to us and for us to enjoy spending some time with her during her convalescence. After her cataract surgery, she was on a strict regime of regular eye drops and care. Through all the handling and treatment, she never resisted or grumbled and proved to be the perfect patient. Janet warned me that when she came home to us in a few weeks' time, she would still require regular eye drops and checks for some while. I couldn't wait to begin looking after her. On each visit she seemed a little less timid and definitely started to respond to Renae and myself with cautious recognition – we no longer seemed strangers to her. Physically she was also continuing to improve as her health was steadily being restored. Her coat, whilst still patchy, was beginning to thicken and her hip bones and ribs were no longer visible as she was gaining a little weight.

Renae loved these visits for each one was a repeat of the first, a proper schnauzer-fest with whoever was visiting Janet for the day or being fostered. On one such visit we met a handsome, cheeky male dog – Crackers – who had spent his days in a puppy farm and was being fostered by Donna. Although a little scared, he was full of mischief and looked less traumatised than some of the other survivors that I had met. I wondered about the different impact for males that being in a puppy farm would have. Donna had fostered several males and in her experience, they are affected as badly as the females but in different ways. They may not experience the same physical demands and risks of pregnancy time after time that the females do, but psychologically they are damaged the same. They too are kept in confinement and isolation, experience the same rough handling and physical abuse and suffer terrible loneliness. Many male dogs are killed because fewer males are needed in order for a puppy farmer to be profitable. Unsold male puppies are less likely to be kept to maturity than their female counterparts.

July came and we headed off on our summer trip with Renae knowing that when we returned, Susie-Belle would be joining our home and we would all begin our new lives together. This was Renae's first overseas trip and Michel and I were excited but somewhat reflective for it was the first visit to France together with a dog since losing Jasmine. Over the years we had made so many trips that it had become second nature for Jasmine to settle down in the car and snooze her way through France as we drove south. We had been sure to get Renae used to car travel since she came to us for we knew that long journeys through France were to be a regular part of her life and so far she had not shown any problems. However, a solid twelve-hour stint in the car would be a good test of her tolerance for long distance travel. As it turned out, we should never have doubted her – she took to the journey like a true professional canine traveller, being completely at ease in the car throughout the trip. Indeed she proved to be a perfect travelling companion and seemed to love her first French holiday.

We cut short our time that summer in France so that we would have more time available to settle Susie-Belle in at home before our regular working lives resumed following the end of our summer break. Whilst we were away I had frequent updates from Janet on how Susie-Belle was doing; her recovery from the cataract operation continued to go well and she had meanwhile been joined by another blind foster buddy – Connie – awaiting the go ahead for cataract surgery. Again I was shocked at how many of these breeding bitches had eye problems which more than likely would one day affect their numerous puppies. I can only hope that the puppies would be in homes where their eyes would receive proper veterinary care and that they would be loved and safe, should they lose their vision. Connie eventually had the operation to restore her sight and recuperated together with Susie-Belle and now lives a very happy life with her cavalier King Charles spaniel brother, Oscar. She does have ongoing health problems including pancreatitis and a deformed leg, which restricts the exercise she can do. Although the cause has never been confirmed it is suggestive of an old fracture that would have been left untreated in the puppy farm, a horrible example of how much the dogs can physically suffer during their breeding captivity. But in her home now, she lives peacefully and safely as beautiful Bella, much loved and receiving all the best veterinary care that she needs to keep her well.

Following rescue, some of the survivors from breeding farms can require a lot of veterinary care, both before and after permanent homes are found for them. This can make them hard to find good homes for. Dee Dee, another of Janet's ex-fosters, experienced similar eye issues to Susie-Belle and in her short life of freedom with her new family had several serious health challenges, including the potentially fatal Cushing's disease and four slipped discs in her spine that required major surgery. The specialist caring for her also found damage to her neck and tail, which, just like Bella, could have been caused by a previous traumatic incident. Despite the illness that Dee Dee suffered in her life outside the battery farm, she did at least end her days in the loving home of her adoptive family and had known a safe, quiet, good existence for the short time she was with them. Sadly this is not the case for so many dogs that end their lives never knowing any love or compassion.

Soon enough our time in France came to an end and rather than the usual end-of-holiday gloom, we were excited to be heading home to our life with Susie-Belle. We arrived back in the UK late one night and the following morning the three of us made an early trip to Berkshire to collect the new, long-awaited member of our family. I knew that for Janet it was going to be an emotional time for she had nursed and loved Susie-Belle for six months. With her patient expert care, Susie-Belle had gone from being a dog too scared to look at anyone, who cowered in fear whenever she was approached, bald, skinny, half blind, to a dog that now looked slender rather than skinny, who allowed Janet to cuddle her without flinching, one whose coat was continuing to improve and perhaps most preciously, one for whom eye sight had been preserved.

I am profoundly moved by the generosity and humanity with which Janet and other fosterers do what they do. To care for dogs that arrive so damaged, so traumatised that it can take weeks before they allow any touch and months of nursing to improve their physical health and then to allow others to continue the journey and enjoy the happy outcome is truly remarkable. The fosterers share their homes and hearts with these dogs, do all the hard work and then let other fortunate families enjoy the new lives that they have made possible. Without the work of fosterers many of the puppy farm survivors would struggle to find homes they could live in forever. There are many people who may consider adopting a dog, but doing so for a dog who has never lived in a home, is not house trained, who cannot walk on a lead, or even allow a lead to be put on, who may never be a normal well-adjusted dog is a particular kind of adoption, one made easier by the preparation offered in the best foster homes.

It had been a few weeks since we'd last visited. Michel and I had a silly moment of anxiety over whether Susie-Belle would remember us or indeed want to come home with us. When we arrived in Janet's office, she looked up from her bed and quietly came forward to say hello first to Renae, followed by a gentle sniff of my outstretched hand. This was as exuberant as we might expect Susie-Belle to be and she settled herself back in her bed, content to observe whilst we completed the formalities and received our final instructions from Janet on how to continue with her eye care. In addition to the drops for the post-surgery care, which we needed to continue for a few more weeks, Susie-Belle had been diagnosed with a further debilitating eye disease: keratoconjunctivitis, commonly known as 'dry-eye'. This requires twice-daily application of expensive eye drops and most likely was something that would require lifelong treatment. We weren't fazed by it, but I did resolve to do my own research once she was home and dependent on us to see what we might do for her in addition to providing her with the correct veterinary treatment to support her eye-health. I had a feeling Susie-Belle's eyes would be an ongoing issue beyond her cataract surgery recovery.

When all the paperwork was done, instructions given and going-home treats gobbled up by Susie-Belle in Janet's office, we headed out to the car with her wearing her new violet harness, walking neatly alongside Renae. Although it was an emotional moment, we were keen not to make too much of a fuss in order to avoid upsetting Susie-Belle. I had promised Janet that I would stay in touch to let her know how we were getting along and would be back to visit from time to time. With hugs all round and not too much delay, Janet said her goodbyes, almost managing to hold back the tears until she waved Susie-Belle off to her new life in the back of the car with Renae, her new sister.

CHAPTER SEVEN

Nocturnal Dramatics

'Remember, remember, this is now, and now, and now. Live it, feel it, cling to it'
– THE JOURNALS OF SYLVIA PLATH, *SYLVIA PLATH*

In her first few days at home with us, Susie-Belle was very quiet but seemed slightly distant rather than withdrawn. She would spend her time sitting in her bed watching everything going on but not particularly engaging with us. Renae appeared to be happy sharing her home and we often found her taking a selection of her toys over to Susie-Belle to see if she wanted to play. She never did – Susie-Belle had no concept of play. Life in a battery farm for a dog is not a life where play is either encouraged or possible. The dogs are usually kept in isolation and even when they have contact with other dogs, their environments are austere. Toys serve no purpose for dogs that are being kept for breeding, or puppies that will be sold to buyers who will never have contact again with the seller if the seller has their way. These are not puppies that the seller or breeder wants to hear any more about, they are not interested in how well – or not – the puppies are getting on in their new homes. They won't want to hear if the cute little puppy turns out to be a poorly one within days of reaching its new home and they are certainly not going to be bothered about ensuring the puppies develop healthy, playful instincts by providing frippery like toys or entertainment. As for the captive breeding bitches and dogs, when their days are about staying alive and coping with the pain they suffer, playing is never going to be something they do much of, even if by some miracle their early years had nurtured this within them.

An obvious and complete unawareness of how enjoyable it is to play was horrible to see in Susie-Belle. We had never been close to a dog that didn't show at least a passing interest in a game, even if it was only fleeting. There was zero reaction from Susie-Belle to Renae's persistent invitations to play. Healthy dogs, even as they grow out of puppyhood and into adult life, usually retain an enthusiasm for play unusual amongst mammals, most of whom typically grow out of it as they enter maturity. It is one of the special connections that humans and dogs share. Humans keep their enjoyment in playing games throughout their life span, be it football, tennis, chess, computer or card games, even when the energy required diminishes with age. Whether from the sidelines or watching on TV, we still want to participate in some kind of game. So do dogs.

Seeing Susie-Belle with a complete lack of interest in playing was sad but it didn't seem to bother Renae. She would drop a ball onto the floor in front of her sister, who would not appear to notice this action, let alone recognise it as an invitation for a game. Squeaky toys, amongst Renae's favourites, didn't register with Susie-Belle. She just did not relate on any level to Renae's joyful play, or cheeky teasing to get involved in her games. Fortunately it didn't worry her sister, who simply turned to the closest alternative: us. We were always happy to oblige and play chase, fetch, throw or tug-the-toy – after all who can resist a playful pooch, apart from a damaged dog whose deprived existence had never awakened this within her? There are canine behavioural and developmental researchers who believe that there is a critical time when play is developed in dogs and for those raised or kept in environments where this is not available, like puppy farms, they may simply never be able to learn how to play with items such as toys or balls.

We decided from the outset that a consistent daily routine would be important to help Susie-Belle settle into her new life and in the first week or so we kept her walks restricted to our local park, close to home. Here we met a regular group of dogs and owners who we knew to be predictable and trustworthy, which we hoped would allow Susie-Belle to explore her new environment in quiet safety. Her emotional stability was fragile and what we didn't want to risk was having an incident early on with either dogs or humans that might frighten her and set her back. As well as Susie-Belle familiarising herself with her surroundings and new home, we were also getting to know her and how to handle her fears and manage her anxieties with traffic noise, sudden loud sounds and movements. Being near home and mixing with friends who understood she was a special case seemed wise.

The first few park sessions involved Susie-Belle sticking close to our heels, head hung low, and keeping out of the way of everyone. At the start she showed little interest in anything and didn't venture more than a few steps from our feet. It was as if she was concentrating hard on not being seen, on not drawing attention to herself. Or, and this is what we liked to joke about to lighten the mood if we thought she looked too worried, that far from being worry-worn, she was practising a uniquely Susie-Belle style of walking meditation and was in fact in a perfect state of inner peace, untouched by any distractions or worries. Either seemed possible as one thing was apparent: Susie-Belle was a dog with a phenomenal amount of concentration and patience, she was definitely patient! In the house she would sit for long periods without moving a muscle to the point where I would feel compelled to wander over and check up on her to be sure she was all right. She would sit and stare into space, or at the floor and be seemingly unaware of anything – nothing seemed to disturb her thoughts when she sat like this. But then we would just catch a little sideways glance from her and know that she was with us, watching, just being.

Although we couldn't know for certain what her life had been, we guessed that in the puppy farm, she would have had very little to do apart from sitting for hours on end. Through necessity, Susie-Belle had adopted a patient acceptance and learned to just be present but not expectant. With all the years of practice she had been forced to endure she was very good at it. It saddened us to think of her sitting alone in a cold impoverished environment so we took comfort from imagining she had learned the art of meditation, achieving a Zen-like state of inner peace amidst the misery that had surrounded her. All utter fantasy on our part, but seeing her quiet and solemn ways whilst out and about as well as in the house, it was easier on our minds to tell ourselves that she was in a practised state of living peace. Of course we knew that it was much more likely that the busy, noisy environment of the normal outside world was rather overwhelming for this frightened little dog and her means of survival involved a careful disengagement from it all until she felt ready to cope.

In the months waiting for Susie-Belle to come home to us, with all my chatter about her to everyone we knew, there was quite a band of eager Susie-Belle watchers awaiting her in our local area. People were genuinely pleased to meet our little dog and as they had all been thoroughly instructed in how I wanted them to behave around her, it wasn't too many days before she started to engage with some of our best dog walking friends. I had lain down some clear ground rules amongst the park regulars: Susie-Belle was not to be directly approached, or ever touched without my approval. Both these actions may be very threatening to her and risked sparking a panic; she was not to be fed any treats by anyone as we needed to establish a clear connection with her and controlling her access to food and treats was a way of helping this process. I tried to discourage people from standing and peering over at her or encroaching her space, preferring to allow her to decide when and with whom she wanted to engage. Despite the need for gentle enforcement of our rules, we were determined to be as calm and confident as we could manage whilst we were out so as not to create any unnecessary sense of tension or worry in Susie-Belle.

When it came to supervising her interactions with dogs, we were delighted to see how Renae straightaway shared this responsibility. The months of socialising and training really paid off now as she was always close at hand if dogs showed interest in Susie-Belle and even if she was busy in the midst of a game with her pals, Renae would come over to check her sister was alright when she spotted a dog in her space. It was beautiful to see how natural and close their bond quickly became. We are certain that Susie-Belle took comfort in having such a committed and vigilant canine sister around to watch out for her and have no doubts at all that Renae helped to rehabilitate Susie-Belle in ways that we could not have managed alone.

All the early encounters thankfully proved uneventful, and with the familiarity of environment, people and dogs, within a short while Susie-Belle started to venture more than inches from our ankles. She was soon stretching her own boundaries, moving a few feet further and subtly began to engage with the regular dogs and humans we met whilst out and about. With every walk she showed less nervousness overall, less agitation when a car sped past, less reactivity to an unexpected encounter with a strange new person wishing to stop and say hello and the jitteriness when a dog bounced up to greet the new girl dropped to near normal levels. We soon got to understand when her anxiety took over – we would find her quickly repositioning herself to tuck once again tightly behind our feet. As the weeks passed, we began walking farther afield and taking her out to different places in the car. With Susie-Belle's new life as one divided between France and the UK, it was essential that she was comfortable with long distance drives and we set about making decent-length car journeys part of her routine. The first major car journey came within a few weeks of being at home with us.

As well as being out and about with my dogs, the other great pastime that I enjoy is outdoor swimming and the arrival of Susie-Belle coincided with the final few events of the open water swimming season for the year. Earlier in the year, before plans for Susie-Belle had taken over my life, I had entered a charity swim event in Devon and had arranged to enjoy the weekend away with a stay in a country inn hotel on the Friday night, followed by the swim on the Saturday morning. All had been planned prior to Susie-Belle's arrival, and we considered cancelling the trip as she had only been with us for such a short while. We worried the sudden change in routine, the long car journey and new places may be too overwhelming but, as she seemed to be settling in well, we stuck with the plan and headed to Devon on the Friday, a few weeks after she began living with us.

We arrived in the West Country in the early evening, having stopped once during the four-hour drive and all appeared to be fine with Susie-Belle, no mishaps or apparent stresses. She had travelled well, sitting with Renae in the back and all looked promising for her first weekend away on the road with us. We had booked a room in a dog-friendly country inn based in what the owners said was the darkest village in England. With no streetlights and being in the depths of the Devonshire countryside, it was indeed dark, pitch black in fact, soon after we arrived. We had brought dog beds and blankets with us to help familiarise Susie-Belle and Renae to their new surroundings. Renae was completely at ease – a confident travelling companion, she was clearly enjoying the excitement of a trip away. Susie-Belle was harder to read; she had been settled in the car and wasn't showing any obvious signs of anxiety. She ate her supper well and after we'd eaten our own in the pub, we set out into the depths of darkness for a final toilet opportunity for the night, wandering along the unlit lane and hoping the dogs did what they needed to do. But Susie-Belle had other ideas and her bladder and bowels were not cooperating. She diligently walked alongside Renae, we shone the torch to see what was going on, but there was nothing to see.

Susie-Belle was not performing in the peace and quiet of the Devonshire night air, which by this stage was feeling ominously chilly for my early morning swim in a lake. But that was a distant worry for me at that stage. Right now, the lack of toilet activity from Susie-Belle was more pressing as I pondered how we were going to manage a need for a pee in the middle of the night, staying in a hotel. I decided that I would leave it to Michel to deal with, should it happen, mentally justifying my secret decision by the need for a good night's sleep in preparation for my cold swim, which was feeling less and less like a good idea as the night chill set in. Eventually after wandering up and down the lane for what was by now getting close to an hour and still no sign of Susie-Belle performing, we called it a night and settled into our room, hoping she would be happy till morning.

At 2am we were woken by the sound of Susie-Belle frantically pacing the room and heavily panting. We had covered the bedroom floor with the dog blankets and my swimming towels just in case of any accidents and as her bowels spectacularly exploded, we were thankful we had. So much for feigning sleep should she need one of us to get up during the night for a wee! Rapid emergency action was needed by both of us and whilst Michel rushed her outside into the night time cold, I frantically set about clearing up, all the while hoping we hadn't woken anyone else staying at the inn, not only because we didn't wish to disturb them, but because it was a distinctly unpleasant and embarrassing experience we had on our hands.

By the time Michel and Susie-Belle came back to the room, the towels and blankets had been bagged and binned and all evidence of Susie-Belle's mishap had disappeared. By now, we were all wide awake and as Renae seemed to think it was time for her day to start, there was little chance of any of us getting much sleep for the rest of the night. I lay awake, ready to spring into action at the first sign of any movement from Susie-Belle, who now appeared to be undisturbed by her earlier diarrhoea dramatics. I remembered that Janet had told me that she had been admitted for treatment by the vet during her time there: haemorrhagic diarrhoea, a serious condition if left untreated. Janet had seen it many times with her foster dogs from puppy farms and believed that it was a clear sign of stress. I wrestled with my thoughts in the depths of the night, felt guilty that we had brought Susie-Belle away too early and wished that we had just cancelled the weekend trip. I worried that my actions would make her seriously ill again and my imagination raced itself all the way to a horrible fate for Susie-Belle by the time I eventually drifted into a fitful sleep.

We woke at dawn and anxiously offered Susie-Belle some breakfast, which she promptly gobbled up and looked for more. She seemed completely fine and not in the least disturbed by her nocturnal accident. We decided against heading home early and carried on with our weekend plans; I completed the swim, which wasn't cold despite the chilly night and the feel of early autumn in the air. Renae and Susie-Belle stood with Michel amongst the spectators, quite happily taking in the sights, sounds and smells of the event, and afterwards we headed to Dorset to stay with a friend for the rest of the weekend. Whilst Susie-Belle's tummy wasn't completely settled, it was nothing concerning and by the time we arrived home late on the Sunday night, she was back to her normal self.

We were glad that we had gone ahead with the weekend away as we were determined that Susie-Belle should have the opportunity to live a richly varied life and do everything with us. But the incident in the middle of the night was a sobering reminder to us that she was a sensitive soul requiring vigilance on our part if we were not to push her too far, too quickly. It was a balance we hoped to get right whilst not causing her any unnecessary health issues in her early days of learning to live her new life. We reminded each other to keep a close watch for signs we may be stressing her in our eagerness to share everything with our special girl, for whom everything was new.

CHAPTER EIGHT

Crowds and a Cool Dip

'Live in the sunshine, swim the sea, drink the wild air'
– 'MERLIN'S SONG', RALPH WALDO EMERSON

After Susie-Belle's stress-induced tummy incident in the middle of the night on her first weekend away we knew that we would have to work carefully to ease her into her future travelling lifestyle if she was to enjoy it and not be stressed each time. Our first visit to France was planned for December and so we decided to expose her to many different experiences and environments in the three months before her big trip across the Channel. Although the temptation was to stay quietly at home in an environment without challenge to keep her safe and free from stress, we felt this would not allow her to fully enjoy the life she could have with us. If we took this easier option in the short term, we ran the risk of inadvertently trapping her in her self-imposed shell, something we hoped she would break free from when she was ready. If we didn't give her the broadest opportunities to experience the good things out there in the wider world, her expectations, of which so far she gave no sign of having any, would not expand and her life as a normal dog would never develop fully.

Much as I felt I easily could, I knew that we needed to avoid smothering Susie-Belle with love and stifling her potential but rather we must do everything to empower her. We wanted her to love living, to thrive now, not to be stuck in the flytrap of awfulness that had gone before in her life. So, we decided we would get Renae and Susie-Belle out and about as much as possible into situations that gave them both the best chance to fill their minds and memories with joy. Susie-Belle's life was no longer to be limited: it would be as rich and perfectly satisfying as one of Michel's finest chocolate soufflés. So I started to plan things to do with her where we could watch out for her emotional responses and change what needed changing to make each day a sweet experience for her.

An event had caught my eye a few months earlier that was to be held in Brighton on the South Coast, just over an hour's drive from us. Pup Aid, a large, celebrity judged fun dog show, was being held to raise awareness of the horrors of the puppy farming industry. The day looked to be a lively mixture of celebrity spotting, fun dog show classes, live music, eating, stalls for shopping and all in the noble cause of shining a spotlight on the murky world of puppy farming. What couldn't we like about it? Founded by TV vet Marc Abraham, the primary aim of the day was to make a contribution to raising awareness amongst the public of the horrible truth behind the breeding of many puppies in the UK. In attracting celebrities, it brought publicity to the issues and created a newsworthy event and we definitely wanted to go along and support the day if we thought Susie-Belle could cope.

We talked it through and whilst it seemed the perfect place to take our own puppy farm survivor in her programme of socialisation and experiences we did have some reservations as to whether it would be a wise thing to expose her to such a busy environment so early on in her new life with us. Eventually after mulling it over and talking ourselves in and out of going, we judged that with the presence of all the dogs in the show this would bring her comfort if she was stressed, and after all we didn't have to stay too long. We wouldn't force her to be there if she wasn't happy and agreed that if she showed any signs of distress, we would bring Susie-Belle home. We would not ignore the reality if she was experiencing significant anxiety and if that meant we came home without getting out of the car then that's what we would do.

The morning air was warmed by late summer sunshine as we arrived at the magnificent Stanmer House, an eighteenth-century mansion on the outskirts of Brighton that was playing host to Pup Aid. Susie-Belle was still very uneasy when people walked behind or close to her. It was going to be a slow process getting her the few hundred yards into the event but I told myself that however long it took, if she could manage it then we would do it as all the time she was taking a few steps forwards and not completely freezing with fear, or shutting down she was progressing. The moment I thought she was anywhere close to being overwhelmed, we would go back to the car and head for home. Making our way down the hill from the car park amongst the building crowds involved a constant series of stops and starts as she paused to let people pass, only to take a few steps forwards, freeze and the same process take over once again. When she stopped, I stopped and would kneel down next to her, giving her chin a reassuring tickle until she was happy to start walking again. Or we'd stand still together, let the people pass and, in her own time, she would decide that as nothing terrible had happened, it was once again safe to take a few steps to catch up with Renae, who was a short distance ahead with Michel.

It was all good experience, for her and for me. I felt it was going a little way towards letting her feel and experience for herself what it may be like to let go of her fears. She was not being forced to do it – I would have happily returned to the car and abandoned our visit had she not shown a willingness to carry on. It was good to see her stretch forwards a little with each step that day to being the dog she was showing faint signs of wanting to be.

The single reason we had decided to go along for the day was to empower Susie-Belle. We wanted to guide her through challenges on a regular basis as that way we believed she might eventually shed her fears and release the normal dog hidden within her. We knew it would take time before she would, or could be herself, but hoped new experiences would help her on her way. Living in the most congested corner of the UK, Susie-Belle had to get used to people walking around her as our day-to-day life involved busy places, and although the volume of people at Stanmer House exceeded what she would come across during an average day, we hoped the exposure would go some way towards dispelling her fears without overwhelming her. I don't know if we got it right or not, as we also recognised that she had not yet been with us very long and to build new positive associations around things she currently feared had to be done within the context of her feeling safe and secure with us. We hoped that she was far enough on that journey for the day to help, not hinder her but we remained watchful for signs we had judged it wrongly.

Whilst Susie-Belle stopped and started her way along the pathway, our slow, faltering pace gave Renae the chance to fully take in the new and exciting sights, smells and sounds all around and politely greet the many dogs who were heading in the same direction. Although excited and keen to join in with the fun, Renae stayed close to her sister, coming back when she got too far ahead. From time to time she appeared to be reassuring her, nuzzling her face close to Susie-Belle's when she stopped once again to let someone past. Not for the first time I silently thanked Renae for being a perfectly patient sister and knew that the help she was giving Susie-Belle, although not properly understood by us, was evidently clear between them and beautifully comforting to observe.

Eventually we reached the entrance to the grounds where Pup Aid was being held and what a sight greeted us. There were dogs and people everywhere and following the endurance feat of making the short journey from the car, my nerves (and not Susie-Belle's) almost failed. I very nearly scooped her up and bolted straight back to the car to drive off to the peace and quiet of home but I reminded myself that this was an event for dogs like her and to raise awareness of what causes the damage that led to her being the way she was. Now we were there, I couldn't take the easy route out and go straight back home, especially as Susie-Belle had just made what for her had been a tremendously brave effort to get through the crowds from the car to the show. We at least needed to have a wander round first and let Susie-Belle and Renae have the chance to enjoy a day out.

Once I'd wrestled with my own anxiety about Susie-Belle being amongst so many people and had taken a few deep breaths, I relaxed, looked around and realised what a fantastic event we were at. The atmosphere was lively but not frenetic and there were plenty of dogs of all shapes and sizes milling happily around. In the show ring, there were rescue dogs competing for Prettiest Bitch, Most Beautiful Eyes and Best Dressed Dog. Elderly dogs with grey muzzles lined up to be the show's Golden Oldies and children proudly led their four-legged friends into the ring for Best Family Friend. Men on stilts wandered around, amusing children and startling the adults. Charity stalls, food stands and vendors selling everything imaginable for dogs spread out across the grounds. Looking at Renae amidst all this it was clear that she was loving the activity, smells, stimulation and attention and whilst we were vigilant with Susie-Belle, we enjoyed seeing Renae take the bustle in her stride and happily interact with dogs and people alike. This could only help Susie-Belle to share in the fun of being a normal dog and one day by a process of familiarisation we hoped she might show almost the same level of pleasure as her sister when taking part in new experiences. I was glad we had come and even more pleased we'd stayed to enjoy it.

Amongst the frivolity and fun, the purpose of the event was ever present with several stalls promoting awareness of puppy farming, small independent charities and organisations displaying pictures of breeding dogs: some rescued, others still captive. Many of the images were horrific – dogs with bent backs and pregnant bellies dragging on the ground, undercover photographs of the terrified faces of breeding dogs looking out of dark, tiny, filthy pens. Dogs surrounded by their litters, lying on grubby sawdust or concrete floors. It was sobering to see these images on a sunny day of joyful activity and remind ourselves why we were there. Up until a few months previously that had been Susie-Belle's life.

After lunch, we headed home but not before we had seen the emotionally moving parade of ex-breeding bitches, all rescued from terrible conditions in puppy farms and now living the kind of lives that all dogs should enjoy – free from pain, suffering and neglect, surrounded by an abundance of love and compassion. As the dogs completed the parade, the physical abuse of their past existences were evident in the grossly distended nipples, huge sagging bellies that had carried litter after litter, the overextended backs strained by carrying multiple pregnancies and the splayed feet from the weight of pregnancies and cramped living spaces. Seeing these damaged dogs was sad but powerfully reinforced the message of the day: amongst the fun and lightness, this was the awareness that the organisers wished people to take home. Buying puppies indiscriminately, ignorantly or just plain naively fuels the demand and continues the abuse of thousands of parent dogs. That night, I gave Susie-Belle an extra-special supper and a gentle cuddle.

With autumn fast approaching we wanted to continue the momentum of Susie-Belle's programme of new experiences, so the weekend following Pup Aid, we took her down to the beach for the first time for what would be my last sea swim of the year. We chose a spot on the South Coast that we knew wouldn't be too hectic, not only for Susie-Belle's sake but also because the day was blustery with an ominously leaden sky and the thought of me stripping off and striding into the water in my swimsuit in front of a bewildered audience of beach walkers huddled sensibly in their warm coats seemed as much of a feat of courage as walking the busy pavements must have been to Susie-Belle. Only Susie-Belle and pavements was a rational enough activity, sea swimming on a chilly day under black skies might appear to be less so to many. The less attention both Susie-Belle and I attracted the better was my overriding hope as I stood wrapped in my coat, looking out towards the grey, murky waters breaking over the shingle. This was almost certainly Susie-Belle's first ever experience of the seaside and she stood at my feet, lifting her face to take in the flood of tastes and smells of the seaside as they whipped themselves around her in what was a much cooler and stronger wind than I had hoped for when we left home that morning.

Tempting as it was just to stroll on the beach letting Susie-Belle savour her new environment, I really did want to get in a last swim before we headed into winter and as Michel stood on the shoreline with Renae and Susie-Belle, I braced myself, took a deep breath and dived into the cool autumnal waves. Much of my enjoyment from outdoor swimming comes from the sheer release of tension it brings and the primal sense of freedom I feel whilst swimming. Nothing worries me when I'm swimming, any stresses I might drag with me into the water don't survive the immersion and I come out refreshed in body and mind. Coming up for air and looking back at Susie-Belle standing on the shingle with her characteristic hunched, tight, tense stance, I wondered when, if ever, she had felt such a feeling of being free as I did in that moment. As she stared out to sea at me, probably wondering what on earth I was doing as I dipped up, over and through the waves, I hoped that she might be able to sense my joy at doing something I loved. As canine researchers now know that a deep level of emotional interplay exists between dogs and their human companions, I felt there was a chance that in some way, Susie-Belle's emotional response to her day at the beach would be positively enriched by my evident enjoyment of a cold, rough sea swim.

If I had thought she would enjoy swimming with me that

day, I would have gladly taken her paw and led her into the sea alongside me, but she was no water-loving Labrador and showed no inclination to come close to the water's edge. However, I was determined one day to find out what she would enjoy and to discover the key to unlocking her from the anxiety and tensions she was currently imprisoned by. As I dived again below the chilly water, a dream of Susie-Belle one day living freely without fear or tension, unshackled from the memories of her past abuse, accompanied me as I swam back to shore.

CHAPTER NINE

Not All Dogs
Like a Stroke

'Let's face it: I'm scared, scared and frozen'
– THE JOURNALS OF SYLVIA PLATH, *SYLVIA PLATH*

We knew that it may take a long time for Susie-Belle to reach a state of relative relaxation where she might start to feel like a normal dog. It would be a process that would take as long as it took and would not, nor could be rushed. Although I had no experience of this kind of intensive rehabilitation work, from reading widely and talking to others who did, I knew that she could only be the dog she could be and we could not rush her. Much as I longed for her to be carefree and not to have a fearful moment ever again in her life, she could not be that dog until or unless she was ready. Although I accepted that it would take whatever time was needed, I really hoped her fear would subside enough to allow her soon to start feeling the love that now surrounded her. The love that would accompany her every single day of her life would keep her safe and if only she let herself sense it, bring her sheer, simple happiness. Whilst my logical mind understood the healing process would be a lifelong journey that we would travel together over many patient years, my inherently impatient nature niggled away and I looked for ways that I might help my special dog in her development.

I have worked as a natural health practitioner for a number of years, professionally practising massage and acupuncture to help heal all manner of physical and emotional problems in my patients. As such, touching Susie-Belle with soothing massage was for me a natural impulse and the easiest, most normal, intuitive thing that I could do with her. However, it was far from easy or normal for her to receive my tactile offerings and to begin with, her little body was tight under my fingers, resistant to any effort on my part to induce a positive response. I had never touched a living thing that felt so tense, whose skin bristled the moment my fingertips made contact. It was completely new territory for me to be massaging a body that did not welcome the contact.

During Jasmine's last couple of years, Alison, a veterinary acupuncturist, had visited our home to give treatment for her arthritis and pain and show me what I could do. Over a number of visits, we had shared experiences and knowledge from my work with humans and Alison from hers with pets. I had gained a working understanding of canine anatomy and the location of acupuncture points compared with what I used with my human patients. Overall, there is little difference between how vets use acupuncture and what I would do for the same conditions in humans. When Susie-Belle arrived, I decided to incorporate into her massage some acupressure, the same as if I was treating a human afflicted by the anxiety and fear that she was. My clinical specialty in acupuncture is an area that has major accompanying emotional issues and on a day-to-day basis I witness profound changes in my patients when given the right care and help through which emotional as well as physical healing occurs. In my mind, I could see little difference in how Susie-Belle might be helped if I worked with her in the same way.

So, I got on and did what came naturally. Initially Susie-Belle lay statue-still under my touch, compliant with what was happening but not relaxing a single cell of her body. However, as my fingers worked along the length of her spine, I gently teased out her many knots of tension. I kneaded along the acupressure points as I went and after a few weeks the surface tension in her muscles softened. Soon I was able to work a bit deeper as her body let go of some of the pain and trauma lodged deep into her very being. The sessions we shared could be as short as a couple of minutes if she wasn't in a receptive mood, or as long as half an hour on a good day. After many weeks of this, the first time she let out a sigh of relaxed pleasure I could have wept with joy at what is for most animals a normal sign of relaxation but which for Susie-Belle was a major indication of progress.

Most of the time, my knowledge of what I was hoping to do with Susie-Belle was based largely on my professional background with humans. Over the years, my career had involved developing training courses in the field, some writing and lecturing and I had a sound understanding of the science underpinning the therapeutic effects of touch on humans. In addition, my training as an acupuncturist added a further dimension to what I hoped to achieve with Susie-Belle. However, since those early days with her, my interest in the specific effects of massage on dogs has grown and what I now realise I was doing was effecting both our stress responses in profound ways. Researchers have found that when humans stroke a dog, both their own and the animal's stress hormones change. In particular, the 'feel-good' hormone oxytocin common in all mammals plays an important role in maternal bonding and is directly influenced by stroking. Numerous studies have shown that when owners stroke their dogs for just a few minutes, the oxytocin levels of both rise, leading to the interesting conclusion that I was getting as much out of massaging Susie-Belle as I hoped she was gaining from the experience. Of course I wasn't aware of this at the time – it just made me feel useful to be able to put my professional skills into practise with my precious, damaged dog.

If I'd realised at the time that I was helping her oxytocin levels to rise, which in turn was helping to calm her fears, for that is one of its major roles, I may have pursued our massage sessions with even more vigour than I did. As it was, I think it did help to move her towards feeling peaceful rather than anxious faster than if I hadn't done it. I hope that our sessions quelled any sense of menace that may still have been lurking in her mind for her emotions became less fear-dominated. At the time, whatever I was doing seemed to be helping her; she was steadily responding to my therapeutic approaches. Now I know more of what was happening internally with her and when I think back to the sessions they seem even more special. Massages that began as an intuitive thing on my part were really doing a lot more for Susie-Belle than I might have thought. As well as reducing anxiety, oxytocin helps to build trust and intimacy and perhaps this accounts for the close emotional interplay that exists between man and dog as the same hormone in both controls the same activity. To be tactile with my pets is the most natural and normal thing for me; I am glad that I allowed my intuitive side to guide me in the early weeks. I had some reservations as to whether I knew enough to do it right, but am pleased that I resisted overcomplicating it and thinking myself out of it. By not worrying about things too much and letting myself transfer skills from my work with humans to helping my dog, I know that I helped her.

I was however lucky with Susie-Belle's inherently passive nature as not all dogs from puppy farm backgrounds would have been so compliant as she was with my tactile approach. Some are so traumatised and deprived of kind human contact that their touch aversion is on a scale that is hard for most pet owners to imagine. These are seriously damaged, highly touch-aversive animals – even getting close enough to attach a lead can take a very long while. When approached they rear up on their back legs, they try to get away, or scuttle under or behind furniture, even when living in quiet, understanding homes with people who understand their special needs. They retreat to their 'safe' places in the home and it is important that they have access to such places and use them to take comfort from. This instinctive reaction, which is terribly upsetting to witness, can take a long time to disappear in dogs gripped by it. Darcie is one such dog and her story is one that I find both inspirational and heartwrenching at the same time.

I first came across Darcie around the same time that I spotted Susie-Belle. She was being fostered through the same organisation that had sent Susie-Belle to Janet and at the time she was living in the north of England. She was described as a very scared dog who would require a very special home, which as it turned out was both an understatement and a long time coming for Darcie. As my life with Susie-Belle took shape, I still checked online regularly to see what dogs were available and needed homes and felt an urge to try and help them all get into homes so they could start living their new lives. Idealistic of me, I know, but a feeling I found hard to ignore even though my time and attention was consumed with Susie-Belle and her needs. By December, Darcie had been moved to another foster home in the south of England not far from us but her listing still spoke of her being extremely nervous and requiring a very special home. I found it impossible to stop thinking about how awfully scared she must still be. In the nine months since leaving the puppy farm and whilst Susie-Belle had passed through Janet's loving home, had her cataract surgery and was making steady progress with us in her new home, Darcie had not found a permanent home and remained as scared as when I had first read about her months before. Her new fosterers wrote of her:

> *Poor Darcie hasn't known any love or kindness in her first 5 years so has found it very hard learning to trust humans. She has come a long way since being rescued and does now allow gentle petting and is happy to take treats but her new owner must understand that they will need to be patient, as only time will heal these scars. Darcie is such a sweet, undemanding little girl – all she needs is a warm bed and food, and a doggy friend and owner to share the rest of her life. Darcie has been waiting such a long time for someone to fall in love with her and offer her a home. If you have room in your heart she really does deserve a chance.*

When I saw Darcie's listing several months beforehand I posted about her on an online forum but nothing had come of it. Having seen the latest from her new fosterer, I reposted with a plea to anyone who knew of any potential home for Darcie to do what they could. It seemed so sad that no one had applied for her and other dogs had come and gone to their new homes whilst she was still waiting. I think my sense of attachment to Darcie arose due to the coincidence of timing in spotting Susie-Belle and seeing Darcie simultaneously, then waiting all summer for Susie-Belle to come to me, only to find that Darcie was still stuck at first base with no home in sight, months after leaving the hell of the battery farm. I had an inexplicable sense of being responsible for finding her a home that I couldn't shake off. Fortunately within a day or so of my online posting, Darcie's luck suddenly, after months of nothing, changed for the better and her perfect home miraculously appeared via the UK Schnauzer Forum. Kathleen, a member of the Forum, had applied to adopt Darcie and although I didn't know her at the time, she lived on the South Coast and was within easy reach of us. I had secret hopes of one day getting to meet the dog that had lodged herself firmly in my conscience.

As it turned out Kathleen and her partner Mel's journey with Darcie was one that I got to see first-hand as having dogs with similar special needs immediately connected us and we soon became real friends, meeting up for walks and sharing the peculiar challenges that Darcie and Susie-Belle presented. I've found that there is a certain understanding that exists between owners of dogs with the kind of background and trauma that comes with puppy farm survivors and there are some things that, until a home is shared with them, cannot be truly understood. In Darcie's case, the major hurdle Kathleen had to overcome was her extreme fear of being touched. Now whilst Susie-Belle held an enormous amount of tension in her body that I could feel as I massaged her, which softened as she gradually relaxed more and more, Darcie would not let Kathleen get anywhere near enough to give her a massage.

Simply approaching Darcie would panic her and she would run round and away from Kathleen, fleeing to be out of arm's reach if she could. Whilst I was following a regular pattern of stroking and massaging Susie-Belle into her new, relaxed life, some days Kathleen was lucky to get a lead on Darcie.

It was only after fourteen months of patience and care that Darcie eventually allowed Kathleen and her family to stroke her without withdrawing or panicking. This was almost two years after leaving the battery farm and starting to live with humans. As I write, Darcie will only now initiate any contact under certain conditions: the cushion has to be placed in the same place on the sofa, Kathleen must avoid leaning too far towards her, nothing can be out of place in her environment otherwise avoidance ensues and so on. Strangers approaching results in all her dramatic stress responses resurfacing and every outing requires vigilance on Kathleen's part but out and about Darcie most certainly goes, and like me, Kathleen is of the view that in the early days, the more outside, normal dog experiences that Darcie had the quicker the healthy dog within started to awaken. Kathleen and her family live close to the beautiful South Downs National Park and Darcie's early walks with her canine sister Schnapps were frequent and invigorating, with plenty of interest to keep any dog amused.

Kathleen believes most of Darcie's healing and progress was achieved through the many stimulating walks they took through the countryside around them. It was where Darcie came alive and as soon as she was capable of being off-lead, Kathleen says she ran free and happy and looked to all to be a normal, healthy, happy dog. Only by seeing her then flinch away when her lead was attached at the end of the walk because of the proximity of humans and physical contact this entailed would anyone realise she was not a normal dog.

Darcie remains a dog with many needs and where she has made progress, there are still major problems that she continues to live with. It may well be that some of the damage will prove permanent. Kathleen suspects that there may be a degree of brain damage, which would not be unusual in a puppy farm survivor. It is most likely that as well as being used as a breeder in a battery farm, Darcie was born there and her mother would have received no assistance in whelping. Puppies have been found suffering from permanent whelping-related problems such as brain damage from oxygen starvation. Darcie, sadly, may be one of them. There are few people who would be willing, or indeed capable of providing Darcie with the kind of safe, patient, loving home that she needs. The effort and dedication that Kathleen and her family have shown is inspiring. At the same time the level of human cruelty, all in the name of profiteering from puppy production that created Darcie's problems and which continues to be inflicted on thousands of animals, remains forever depressing to me.

CHAPTER TEN

Susie-Belle Finds Her Voice

'A bird doesn't sing because it has an answer, it sings because it has a song'
– I KNOW WHY THE CAGED BIRD SINGS,
MAYA ANGELOU

As a natural health practitioner my inclination was to search through the professional world in which I had worked for nearly two decades for assistance for Susie-Belle. Whilst I kept telling myself that the process could not be rushed as she would heal in her own time, I did want to make sure I offered her all I had access to, to facilitate this. A few years beforehand, we had rehomed an extremely nervous cat that had spent almost a year in a cat sanctuary before we came along. Rosie arrived, highly nervous and aggressive towards Jasmine. After living with Rosie terrorising Jasmine for a few weeks with no improvement I decided to investigate whether homeopathic veterinary care would offer us any solution to Rosie's aggression. I took her along to the homeopathic vet who had successfully treated Jasmine as a youngster when she developed a seasonal skin problem. His assessment of Rosie had been perfect and he'd sent us away with three tiny pills to be given at intervals and to return if there was no improvement. Although working in the natural health field, I have to admit to not really grasping how homeopathy works but after witnessing the overnight change in Rosie following the first pill, I didn't care how it worked. Her aggression and bullying of Jasmine stopped instantly and her nervousness began to improve and continued to do so to the point where we had no more problems and a return to the vet wasn't needed. It truly could be described as miraculous healing.

I had forgotten a lot of this until Susie-Belle came to us and I began my search for ways to help her and then remembered Mr Coode and his amazing white pills. It was worth a try – at worst I'd be wasting my money on a consultation – so I headed over to his practice, optimistic that he might be able to offer some help. In the UK it is illegal for anyone other than a Royal College of Veterinary Surgeons-registered vet to prescribe homeopathy for animals and Mr Coode works both as a conventional and homeopathic vet and I trusted that he would tell me how he saw things from both perspectives. Despite my eagerness to try all avenues, I had confidence that if he didn't think he could offer any help, then that would be it and I wouldn't be bumped into a long round of pointless treatment when the best remedy of all was time and patience.

The journey to Mr Coode was quite a drive from our home and on the day of the appointment, it took longer than I expected so we arrived with only a minute or two to spare. This meant that I didn't have enough time to let Susie-Belle explore her surroundings when she got out of the car and when we got to the entrance of the building she refused to enter. She firmly sat down on her haunches at the doorway and would not cross the threshold. I gently tugged at her lead, made soothing sounds, encouraged and cajoled, but no, she wouldn't budge. She had done this before when I had tried to get her into a shop with me and I had learned no matter how long I waited, if Susie-Belle didn't want to move, move she wouldn't. Schnauzers are renowned for their stubbornness, and couple this with a dog with clearly the patience of Job and I knew that she could outwait me any day. I kicked myself for cutting things fine and not allowing more space for her to settle and for me to get her through the door in her own time. If we were to see Mr Coode some time that day, I had no choice so I knelt down, gave her a feeble, please-forgive-me smile, muttered some reassuring words and scooped her up, whereby she promptly flung her front legs out stiffly to each side, arched her back and threw her head back in a rigid posture of fear. That was how we walked into the building together.

It seemed pointless putting her on the floor as we'd go through the whole performance again of her solidly not wishing to move an inch when we were called, so we sat in the waiting area, Susie-Belle's stiff body firmly on my lap. Holding Susie-Belle in that moment, I appreciated for the first time the full meaning of what being scared stiff truly is. Her reactions to being picked up were always the same – widely splayed limbs in a posture of complete terror, body held rigid; eyes wild. Despite gradually getting used to my stroking massages that we did all the time, her fear at being picked up remained as terrible as ever. It would be some months before this began to ease. I did what I could to relax myself with the unyielding body of Susie-Belle in my arms, breathed deeply and calmly, whispered what I hoped were soothing sounds in her ear and gently stroked her back. I'd like to say that she relaxed, but if she did, it was fleeting as we were soon called and fear at going into yet another new room overcame her and she shook dramatically in my arms. I was annoyed with myself for not allowing enough time for us both to deal with the new environment properly.

Mr Coode immediately focussed in on the scared bundle on his treatment table. She crouched, only slightly trembling now, body held tight, head hanging down to avoid eye contact with both humans in the room. It was obvious that she was completely terrified and worse, her response was one well practised: hunker down, cower and make herself as small and unobtrusive as possible. With any luck it would all soon be over. It was heartbreaking to see her learned behaviour manifest so plainly in a place where, if only she knew it, nothing but love and care was present.

Mr Coode's approach is quite distinct from any other vet that I have known and in his calm, gentle way he asked me a series of questions whilst observing and sensing Susie-Belle's body. Homeopathic consultations are very different from regular ones, usually being longer and concentrating not only on the obvious problem, but also searching for other signs or symptoms that may be present. A unique feature is the depth of information on past issues that a homeopathic vet seeks to find out and with Susie-Belle this was obviously difficult. I provided as much information as I could, both from the short time that she had been living with us, but also from things that Janet had told me. The more details Mr Coode had to work with, the better he would be able to help her. I described as fully as I could her behaviour and personality as best I currently understood it, what seemed to trigger particular anxieties on top of the perpetual anxious state she lived in. In turn he asked me questions on her reactions to people and things, changes in routine, and I spoke about my timid little dog for almost an hour with him. In an odd way I found it cathartic to describe her – it seemed to help me to express my thoughts and concerns and as I spoke, I properly realised for the first time the full depth of my feelings for this traumatised dog. I would do anything to protect her, give all I could to help her, and soothe her mind and body in any way she needed.

Once he'd asked me all the questions he had to and silently mused for what seemed an age, what Mr Coode said next took me aback and before I could stop it, my eyes filled with tears. He told me that he considered the most important thing to do for Susie-Belle was to help her address and let go of the crippling grief that she was suffering. This shocked me for it wasn't something that I was expecting to hear – I had just not considered that she may be afflicted by such a painful and disturbing emotion. I'd been so caught up in thoughts around her obvious fear reaction that I hadn't gone beyond this to look at her full psychological picture. It was awful to realise that she was suffering such sadness and had been for so long. Trying to get my own thoughts clear, I asked him to explain his thinking. In his view, to live for years the way she had, being used to breed litter upon litter, to care for her puppies only to have them suddenly removed, probably too early, then to be left all alone and to have gone through this experience as many times as she had, she would have suffered enormous feelings of loss and bereavement again and again. It was so obvious when he explained it, but so easily overlooked when her fear response was most apparent.

At one time, the idea that a dog may feel emotion would

have been considered nonsense. However, it is well established now in the scientific literature that they most certainly do. University departments and journals abound where the subject of canine psychology is studied and published, along with websites with academic as well as popular themes. Anyone who has ever lived with a dog knows they are emotional creatures. Even if our understanding of their emotions may be rudimentary or muddled, we know they have them. It's nice that science now recognises this, but it isn't really surprising. In Susie-Belle's case, although in itself giving birth to a litter of puppies and having them leave her should not introduce disturbing emotional responses as it is part of the normal mammalian cycle of life, the nature of how she would have experienced this made it far from normal or healthy. Dogs like Susie-Belle are confined in appalling conditions to breed, they receive little or no care and they struggle to nurture their puppies – several may die through the course of their breeding years, then those that do survive are taken away and the breeding mum is then left once again in total isolation, until the next time. This distressing world is what Susie-Belle had endured for years. Of course she was experiencing sadness and grief. For me, the afternoon spent in Mr Coode's clinic was enlightening and I was so thankful for his insight. I left feeling that even if the homeopathic remedy he gave me made no difference to Susie-Belle at all, my understanding of her suffering had broadened and this alone was helpful as I could now approach our future together with this in mind.

In the following days I gave her the homeopathic pills as prescribed. I wasn't expecting any major changes to occur, accepting that Susie-Belle's problems had lifelong roots. We did, however, notice subtle signs of her growing confidence and ease within the home, which sceptics may say would have occurred irrespective of the homeopathy. Whatever the trigger for the change, she was definitely changing and for me, the proximity to the introduction of the homeopathy seemed too much of a coincidence to be dismissed lightly. It didn't matter either way, we were just glad good things were happening. She began to interact with us whenever we initiated contact. One morning we got an awkward, stiff little dance with a slight wagging of her docked tail when her breakfast was being prepared. She showed signs of wanting to be almost, but not quite fully, playful with Renae, bumping her bottom into Renae when she half danced around. This was amazing, an action that is so normal, so common amongst dogs, but which had been completely absent till that moment with Susie-Belle. We dared to hope that she was letting some of her trauma go and starting to live in each joyful moment for the first time in her life.

A day or so following her morning dance, we were out in the park in the afternoon near a skateboard area full of children having lots of noisy fun. Up until that point, the unpredictable sounds coming from the space meant that we had given it a wide berth with Susie-Belle, preferring to be cautious rather than regretful if she had reacted badly. However, as we went to move away from the skateboarding, Susie-Belle let out a series of lively barks, woofing her head off as we moved past the children and their boards. This was the first time that she had barked outside the house and it was a sound to treasure. To my ears that afternoon she was singing from her heart – a big, beautiful slowly mending heart that was feeling ready to accept the richness of what life now offered her. From that day on, she had well and truly found her voice and barked her way round the park whenever she felt like doing so and we loved it. Every time she started we laughed as it was so uplifting to hear her express herself. She had a funny guttural bark, quite unlike Renae's or Jasmine's, who both had much higher pitched voices. We darkly joked that Susie-Belle had a gruff, worn-out bark from all the barking she had done in captivity, where no one was around to hear her apart from the other dogs.

> *I know why the caged bird sings, ah me,*
> *When his wing is bruised and his bosom sore,*
> *When he beats his bars and he would be free;*
> *It is not a carol of joy or glee,*
> *But a prayer that he sends from his heart's deep core.*
> – 'SYMPATHY' *PAUL LAURENCE DUNBAR*

We loved to hear Susie-Belle bark, despite our past experience with a noisy schnauzer and doing all we could to train Renae not to give full force to that side of her character. With Susie-Belle it was a real sign of her expressing herself and we did nothing to curb it. We didn't care for a moment if anyone didn't like to hear her singing out to them – we loved it and relished seeing her with her head held high, projecting her voice far and wide, happily free. There was no anxiety or frustration in her bark; it was simply her enjoying herself, every small detail of her body language cried out in support of this. Her head was up, her tail was up and her eyes shone bright. No one could doubt this was a schnauzer that liked trying out the sound of her own voice in her happy new world.

We will never know for certain whether the homeopathy released her ability to express herself vocally and helped her to find her bark. It doesn't really matter but my understanding of grief and severe emotional trauma in humans is that in many traditional healing systems, the voice and self-expression are intimately linked to the emotion of grief. Vocalising is something humans are often encouraged to do in order to move forward from trauma and if I took this understanding with Susie-Belle, her sudden discovery of her bark when out and about was a wonderfully positive step in the right direction.

It wasn't that she didn't bark when she first arrived in the home with us, she did. She barked inside the house, but this new, noisy Susie-Belle was something different. Her post-homeopathy bark was a lot more musical, more animated and somehow more expressive. And it was heard at its best when we were outside the safe environment of the house. We took it very clearly as a sign of her increasing confidence in her own identity. I liked to believe her sadness was dissipating and she was starting to leave her awful memories behind her. Certainly hearing her bark at anyone and anything she wanted to is a sound I never wish not to hear. Not that I was keen for Renae to get any ideas about joining in, the thought of two noisy schnauzers was not appealing. So we reserved our laissez-faire approach to barking purely for Susie-Belle, attempting to maintain some degree of control over Renae's vocal expressions. Needless to say, we frequently failed and continue to do so. More often than not these days, Renae is heard taking a merry part in Susie-Belle's canine choir.

CHAPTER ELEVEN

Food Glorious Food

'We can change the way we make and get our food so that it becomes food again—something that feeds our bodies and our souls. Imagine it: Every meal would connect us to the joy of living and the wonder of nature'
– THE OMNIVORE'S DILEMMA, *MICHAEL POLLAN*

As time went on Susie-Belle settled comfortably into our lives and started to show increasing signs of being more at ease inside the home. When she had first arrived she spoke volumes by simply sitting, sitting and waiting, patiently doing what it appeared she had always done: she sat and she waited. Where some ex-breeding dogs are gripped by a nervousness that makes them alarmingly skittish and hard to handle, fleeing into corners or behind the furniture in their panic, Susie-Belle was the opposite. She simply sat quietly on her bed and watched and waited. Sometimes she would appear to be staring at something we couldn't see, at other times she would just sit back on her bottom, not appearing to want to lie down. She would sit and sit, and as her body grew tired, her shoulders slowly slumping, her head tipping gently forward, seemingly about to lie down and fall asleep suddenly just as we thought she would give in and flop, she would straighten her shoulders, pull herself upright and sit all over again.

I couldn't understand why she wouldn't lie down in comfort and allow herself to rest and relax, deep in her cushioned bed until a friend said it was as if she had no familiarity with a feeling of physical relaxation and so didn't recognise this was something she could do. Sadly, she had to learn that being comfortable in a relaxed position was a good feeling. If she had come from one of the many battery farms where dogs only have concrete floors to lie on, it easily explained why slouching down on a soft, plump bed seemed a challenge for Susie-Belle. When she did sleep she lay with her arms and legs tucked tight underneath her body, her head resting between her front paws just poking out enough to act as support, but never laying on her side. We didn't realise the oddity of this sleeping position until months after she had been with us. One evening we saw her flop down on her bed in a truly relaxed state and drift off to sleep in a normal side-lying position for the first time.

An early sign we did spot of Susie-Belle openly starting to feel comfortable in the home was in her eagerness to participate when we were preparing meals, whether it was ours or Renae's and hers. Whilst most of the time when we weren't out on a walk Susie-Belle would seem content to sit in her bed, as soon as activity in the kitchen began she became noticeably engaged and keen to take part in the process. It wasn't long before we could predict that within seconds of going into the kitchen around their dinner-time, we would find Susie-Belle either sitting or standing in the kitchen, watching what was going on. It seemed that the key to getting her to engage keenly with us was through food. The moment she arrived, she had shown a good healthy appetite and as soon as we recognised the obvious enjoyment that she derived from food, we employed it in our efforts to bring her out of her shell.

It was a stroke of good fortune for Susie-Belle that she landed in the home of a professional chef, who, contrary to what many often assume, loves nothing more than cooking for us at home after his day in the kitchen at work. There is always culinary activity in our house to entertain Susie-Belle and keep her mentally engaged. In the early days with us, she showed real enjoyment when it came to her gourmet life. Whereas most of the time she appeared content to stay quietly tucked out of the way seemingly lost in her own thoughts, when food was around we saw a side to her that brought her fully into our world. Her patient qualities meant that she would sit at our feet when food preparation was going on and not move an inch for as long as it took to gain a morsel, or we left the kitchen. We found ourselves stepping over her and moving carefully around her quiet, determined body sat fully in the centre of the kitchen so we couldn't overlook her. It was the only time we could say that Susie-Belle didn't mind having anyone stand behind her, or walk around her; her determination to be a fully-fledged member of our kitchen corps was consistent and amusing.

Michel decided at the outset that he was never going to feed either Susie-Belle or Renae whilst he was in the kitchen as that way lay a lifetime of behavioural nightmares involving lots of canine begging. So I'm responsible for all their feeding and I do it away from the kitchen but that hasn't fooled Susie-Belle: she knows full well where and with whom the food originates.

Once she had decided the kitchen was a good place to sit if anyone was in it, she never broke from her determination to tempt Michel to break his own rules. Every time he's there, she's there, sat at his feet. Only on the rarest occasion when we've been out walking for the day and arrived home all exhausted does her determination start to crack and she may retreat to her bed, but always only ever after first having a hopeful go at food tasting in the kitchen.

Food preparation for our dogs is as important to us as our own meals. We don't feed them commercially prepared foods, preferring to tailor-make meals and source good fresh food regularly. I don't know if Susie-Belle would have shown quite such eagerness in her mealtimes if we were offering her the same pre-prepared food daily. Certainly the few seconds it would take to tip out a portion of dried kibble into a dish for Susie-Belle would have saved her the effort of waiting for us to prepare her dinner, but on the other hand, we would have all missed out on the many moments of warmth and joy that her flourishing interest in food provided early on.

We don't believe that all commercial pet food is bad, but we don't believe it would bring our dogs much joy. Commercially prepared dog food serves a function, but that's not enough of a reason for us to rely on its convenience. We want our pets to know the full pleasure that is to be had when their omnivorous taste buds are tempted with the broadest range of flavours they can experience. I know some may see this as distinctly weird and the amount of thought that we put into providing them with the best meals we can does border on obsessive but for this I make no apologies. Early on, mealtimes became times of abundant pleasure for Susie-Belle without doubt and for a dog that has known real starvation any obsession on my part might be forgiven, I would hope. The first signs of true personality hatching from her protective shell came through her relationship with food and how we approached it with her. We know there are many dogs with backgrounds like hers who do just fine on regular, commercial food, but seeing the unrestrained emotional expression that food triggers in Susie-Belle we are pleased that by feeding her the way we do, it has encouraged an aspect of her personality to shine that may have remained lost had we not.

When we had Jasmine, we fed her a homemade diet her entire life, which turned out to be a long and healthy one. Although we take the view that feeding pet dogs doesn't have to be complicated – after all they have evolved pretty well without relying on 'scientifically proven' commercial foods, or mind-boggling nutritional knowledge – I was keen to know that, with Renae, her nutritional needs as a growing puppy were being properly met by what we fed her, so I put my mind to researching this in more depth. Using the knowledge I collated from both these efforts and my existing under-standing of nutrition, I was happy that the way we fed Renae was perfect for her long-term wellbeing.

During the course of my research into canine nutrition I came across a wealth of interesting ideas, controversies and even what seemed to me peculiar ways of thinking about how dogs should be fed. It appeared that what we had been doing for years with Jasmine, based on little more than common sense and our own enthusiasm for food, was reflected in a growing movement geared towards feeding dogs a natural diet. There are a plethora of internet sites and groups devoted to discussing the ins and outs of dogs' daily meals, whole books have been published to instruct on both what to feed and importantly what to avoid. This seems to be a fiercely debated topic, both amongst proponents of natural feeding in its various guises and those hostile to dogs eating anything other than commercial pet food.

As I looked into the subject more, I could see that the feeding of our dogs can be a controversial topic for many people, vets included and I felt thankful that it had never come up for discussion during Jasmine's life with our own excellent vet. As food is so much a part of our family life, if I had been advised, or worse still felt pressurised into feeding Jasmine the same dried food, day in, day out, this would have created problems, as I know that we would not have been able to agree to it. As I delved deeper into the topic, I was confident that with my increased knowledge of what I was doing, we could use food therapeutically with Susie-Belle. I saw it as a fantastic way to promote her recovery from the terrible demands her body had undergone in the battery farm as well as to satisfy the budding gourmet that she was becoming.

Although some vets are either ambivalent or even hostile to pet owners feeding their animals anything other than commercially produced foods, which are often sold by the vets themselves, there are those who actively encourage, or at least support owners who wish to do things differently. Mr Coode, our homeopathic vet, is an advocate of raw feeding, a fact I only discovered when I looked at the rawfoodvets.com website and found him listed. A look through that site gives many reasons why feeding Susie-Belle and Renae the way we do is a completely healthy thing to do. Often described as a BARF style of feeding, what we give them is 'biologically appropriate raw food' – in other words, we feed them what they would get if left to their own devices, or as dogs always did before commercial dog food was available and became thought of as the only way to feed. We feed as nature intended and what their digestive systems are designed to thrive on, which is a variety of raw meat, raw (definitely not cooked) bones and small amounts of plant material in the form of herbs, vegetables and fruits, mainly berries. This is not a radical concept, but it has become controversial in the face of the commercial interests behind the manufacturing of pet foods and the influence they have over the guardians of our pets' health – the veterinary profession. Vets often have little specific instruction on nutrition during their training and with everything else they must learn it is easy to see how relying on the easily available, apparently perfectly balanced and convenient products sold as pet food is an attractive way of approaching dietary advice.

There are many assertions made on both sides of the debate about the quality of what goes into pet food. Producers claim all kinds of positive benefits to feeding their brand of food whilst critics cite evidence of all kinds of nasties being used in their manufacture. Proponents of raw feeding argue amongst themselves about what's needed; for example whether fruit and vegetables would be eaten by dogs in the wild. There are those who follow a 'prey model' where whole prey are fed – skin, fur, guts, the lot – whilst others rely on the convenience of commercially prepared raw food meals from small producers. It can be a confusing and emotive topic, but essentially, dogs are carnivores with systems designed to eat small prey like birds, rats, rabbits and so on, bones included. Their digestive tract is short and unlike humans their saliva doesn't break down food – this happens in the very strong acid of the stomach, where bones, along with everything else, are digested. For digestion to work well, bacteria and enzymes that are abundant in raw meat are needed; cooking meat destroys these and therefore raw is preferable.

In all the reading I did in the early days of finding out as much as I could about canine nutrition and picking my way through the many controversies and debates, what I always kept coming back to was that Michel and I love thinking about, planning and preparing food, both for us and our pets. It would give us no satisfaction just to tip out a handful of biscuits or open a can every day. As I tried to get a clear view of the evidence on all sides, in the end I really decided that we want to enjoy feeding Susie-Belle as much as she enjoys eating what we provide. One objection people sometimes make to home preparing food rather than using packaged meals – both their own as well as their pets – is that it takes time to plan and prepare and it is expensive. Our experience is that it is not expensive with a bit of planning. In any case, we see little as being more important than to give both ourselves and our dogs a good healthy home prepared diet: for us it is the foundation of health, simple as that.

We devote a bit of extra time to planning our weekly diet and happily extend this to Renae and Susie-Belle. Any effort we spend preparing their meals and homemade biscuits is repaid a thousand times in the abundant pleasure they both gain from their food, especially Susie-Belle. We know the treats are healthy for we know exactly what goes into them; these are no chemical artificial concoctions masquerading as food. If we're able and happy to feed fresh beef, chicken, lamb, fish or whatever else is available, who could argue with any credence that this is something we should not do? There is no way, despite whatever claims are made by the manufacturers, that a tin of dog food, or a bag of dried kibble – even a very expensive one– is going to contain the quality of food that we feed Renae and Susie-Belle.

The one area that I struggled to be clear on and wanted to be very sure was correct for us to do was the feeding of bones.

With Jasmine we had never done this on a regular basis; she had the occasional recreational bone but not as a regular part of her diet. As I got more involved in the BARF ways of feeding and understood a lot more about what kind of bones are safe and which ones to avoid we steadily moved fully into feeding a good range of raw meaty bones. I did not enter this realm lightly, having heard like many people the tales of bones being dangerous for dogs. Cooked bones are never safe, others like the weight-bearing ones I avoid in preference to ribs and small carcasses with bones that are soft enough to crunch without splintering. The joy with which Susie-Belle tackled her first crunchy duck neck was a sight that made us both deeply happy and one we enjoyed over and over those first few months she was with us; it is something we still love being a part of with her. She hasn't lost the excitement and appreciation, nor have we and this is one of the major reasons we raw feed her and will never be persuaded to do otherwise – Susie-Belle would never forgive us!

Above: After several months with us, Susie-Belle's anxieties grew less and less as she learned to trust us.

Below: Susie-Belle testing the cold waters of a mid-winter river gave me hope that she would join me in my summer swims.

Above: Susie-Belle and Renae visiting London for the first time.

Below: The first time Susie-Belle saw Janet again after leaving her foster care was in the New Forest on the first ex-foster dog reunion walk we arranged.

Above Left: At the New Forest reunion walk, Susie-Belle and Whisp met. Perhaps this was a reunion for them, as they share many characteristics and health issues and they may be related.

Above Right: Rather than shivering in a freezing barn when the snow fell, Susie-Belle's first winter with us saw her swaddled in a warm winter coat so that she could carry on enjoying her walks and freedom.

Below: Susie-Belle and Michel taking a rest during the first National Schnauzer Walk in the Peak District, May 2012.

Above: Renae and Susie-Belle have been close companions and great friends from the start.

Below: Once Susie-Belle learned to trust us, she then began to accept all we could offer her and the comforts of home.

CHAPTER TWELVE

Reunion

'I felt my lungs inflate with the onrush of scenery—air,
mountains, trees, people. I thought, This is what it is to be
happy'

— THE BELL JAR, *SYLVIA PLATH*

I t was always important to me that when Susie-Belle came to
live with us, we would acknowledge her rough background
and be mindful of the damage this had caused but we would
also not allow this to stifle her potential growth with us.
Before she came along, through all my hours of preparation
and talking to people with experience of the horrors of puppy
farming, I found I had times when it weighed heavily with me
what suffering she would have endured. But, by committing
myself to loving and caring for Susie-Belle for the rest of her
life, I knew that to do this properly, I could not dwell on her
past suffering. Michel and I promised each other that we

would not pity her: we would love her deeply and care for all her needs. But for her to thrive, pity was not permitted. If either of us ever found ourselves slipping into it, we promised to purge those thoughts and pull ourselves together. I want to love her for the dog she is, not for her past sufferings. To be the person that she needed me to be, I also pledged not to allow myself to be distracted by the deep anger that I feel towards those who had wilfully caused Susie-Belle and so many other dogs years of pain, suffering and sadness. Although I strongly believe that all who take part in the wicked battery farming of puppies are cruel and readily deserve my anger, I could too easily be consumed by it if I allowed myself to travel that path. Instead, I committed myself to doing all I could to ensure that Susie-Belle had a life worth living, not just a life lived.

A major part of this has been to give Susie-Belle as many wonderful experiences that a dog can enjoy as we can. I set my mind to making up for all the years of boredom, isolation and loneliness that had been inflicted on her by making every day rich with new memories. Seeing how she seemed to cope well enough with her big day out at Pup Aid shortly after joining us, I felt we could build on this and keep trying out new things with her. Alongside keeping to a daily routine of times for meals, walks, rest and so on which allowed us all to gain confidence, I was sure that if we offered Susie-Belle lots of new experiences the good memories would help the bad to fade. We were very clear that we would not replace one limited existence with another by keeping her within the boundaries of our local environment, which for any dog becomes boring day after day. Instead we committed to getting her out to new, dog-friendly places as often as we could, as well as giving her the familiarity of our local walks to continue to boost her confidence. We hoped a programme of gently stretching her, coupled with the emotional comfort of familiarity would stimulate her senses and build a sense of anticipation and expectation.

I was keen to reunite her with Janet and her pack of schnauzers for a walk so that Janet could see how well she was doing and Susie-Belle could get to see her foster mum once again. Patti, the blind foster dog that had undergone her cataract surgery and recovery with Susie-Belle, now lived in the beautiful New Forest – a perfect place to arrange a group walk – so I set about getting something organised a couple of months after Susie-Belle had joined us. With a bit of networking on the online schnauzer forum, very soon there were around twelve ex-puppy farm schnauzers that Janet and her friend Donna had at some stage fostered eager to join the walk, as well as plenty of other dogs and their owners keen to come along. It was shaping up to be a great reunion walk and as details were finalised, we all hoped the autumnal weather would be kind.

When the day came, there was a light early frost but the forecast was for a bright, dry day and as we drove west and sped through the landscape of open heath and ancient woodland that makes up the New Forest, the sun really came out to join the party. By the time we arrived, it was unseasonably warm. We had arrived in good time and parked up to wait but it wasn't too long before we were joined by our first schnauzer, for along came Whisp. Although I had never met Whisp as she had been adopted from Janet before I first went to visit Susie-Belle, I had heard a lot about her. Janet is convinced that she and Susie-Belle are related, possibly sisters, as they are so similar in personality and appearance and shared many behavioural traits whilst being fostered. Along with Susie-Belle, Whisp is one of Janet's longest-staying fosterers as when she was rescued from the puppy farm she had multiple health needs and required months of veterinary care before she could be considered for adoption. Through the months she was with her, Whisp stole a tiny piece of Janet's heart and her tale is best told by Catherine, who adopted her a few months before Susie-Belle arrived to fill the place she left in Janet's affections:

When Whisp first arrived out of the puppy farm she was completely shut down: she was unresponsive, totally blind, almost without fur and was so swollen she looked pregnant. She was named Whisp as she only had faint traces or whisps of fur due to an appalling state of mange. Her swollen belly was a womb infection and she had cataracts in both eyes.

Thank goodness for Janet and the Diana Brimblecombe Animal Rescue Centre. Janet fostered Whisp and arranged for her to be seen by the ophthalmologist, who treated the cataract in her left eye but was unable to treat the right one. It took months of veterinary treatment to address Whisp's skin condition and her other health issues and it was over seven months before we could adopt her.

With us, her skin continued to be a problem and our vet treated her for almost a year but it never seemed to fully clear. It was only after many months that we happened to notice and mention that her right eye was red that alarm bells started ringing. She was diagnosed with glaucoma, which unfortunately did not respond to the eye drops and she had to have her eye removed. At the same time, tests on her thyroid revealed hypothyroidism, which had undoubtedly been causing her bad skin. She was started on medication for this once her eye was removed. She was very poorly for a few days after her operation and I shall never forget the night we brought her home, after the operation. She always sleeps on her armchair at the end of my bed and I woke up to find her lying against my tummy, making crying noises. I cuddled her up and stroked her until she went to sleep. I felt so honoured that she had come to me for comfort. Once the medication started working, she became a different dog, and is now a lively, happy dog with a thick normal coat and no more skin problems. We love her so much.

When Susie-Belle and Whisp met in the car park, whether they knew one another or not, we cannot be certain but they did seem to connect, each gently appraising the other in their calm and natural greeting. They were beautifully at ease and to all of us observing, the scene had an unmistaken serenity about it. This would not describe the greetings shared when the rest of the schnauzers started appearing. The rising level of canine excitement was directly matched by an increase in decibels as car after car opened to release yet another schnauzer. It was an overwhelming sight, seeing so many in one place all pleased to see each other and to tell the world for miles around that the schnauzers were in the New Forest that warm and sunny autumn Sunday. After a frenzy of noisy meet and greets, we rapidly decided the best way to deal with the rising excitement and noise was to get the dogs moving and walk. With noses down and bottoms in the air, the dogs set off. As soon as we started to leave the car park, peace descended as the dogs began doing what they do best: checking out the smells of the forest and contributing their own unique aromas.

I had been watching to see Susie-Belle's reaction to Janet as this was the first time that they had been reunited since she had left her care. It was so touching to see immediate recognition from Susie-Belle and her clumsy, awkward mouthing that she only did to a very few select people, Janet of course being one. This action is one that over time has become a lot gentler, but when she first started doing it to me, she would chew on my hands with her characteristic determination as a delightful but almost painful demonstration of her excitement. The trouble was, that as a puppy learns to inhibit their bite when doing similar in play, Susie-Belle had no bite inhibition, but did have the same natural excitement as that which drives a puppy to play bite. In the early days as it was one of the rare signs of her being excited and playful, it seemed wrong to inhibit it or interfere with her emotional expression. So my hands would get chomped at and I would know that when she did this, she was expressing pleasure, the free display of which more than made up for any discomfort I may have suffered for the joy of knowing what lay behind her excitable hand chewing always made me smile. As she has grown into the happier, more emotionally stable dog that she is today, she can still manage to give my hands quite a mangling if she gets carried away. I see any joyful expression in Susie-Belle as a good reason to celebrate with her and usually give her jaws something else to chew on – dried venison trachea often substitutes for my fingers. Her happy displays always get rewarded without hesitation.

As we headed en masse across the heathland, a trail of schnauzers and humans filling the landscape, I had a rough count up of how many dogs were out that day. It seemed that there were around thirty-five, with just under half of them having survived the hideous puppy breeding industry. Seeing them together, in all their damaged beauty but still surviving, I was deeply moved. Six of the schnauzers had undergone cataract surgery whilst in Janet's care, some had been blind and now had sight, there was one with a missing leg and most were overcoming crippling fear. For all of them they had for so many years just existed – by any normal measure it could not be said that they had lived their lives. Though they had been alive, surviving, they had not lived in any sense beyond breathing and breeding. Sharing the simple enjoyment of being out with them all that sunny, warm afternoon and seeing them run round and be the dogs that they should always have been is a memory that I will doubtless never forget. As my stiff, slow Susie-Belle plodded along at the back of the crowd, others were hurtling themselves along the walk, running to and fro between us all – the puppy breeding survivors mingling seamlessly with the normal, privileged pet dogs like Renae, who in her thoughtful way kept coming to the rear to check on her sister. About halfway round the walk, Janet and Donna sat on a carved wooden log seat, surrounded by their ex-foster dogs, all crowding in for attention and cuddles and to soak up the abundance of freedom and love that suffused the day. To see how their foster dogs were now living normal lives in regular homes must have moved Donna and Janet deeply. They are truly wonderful human beings who give so much to the dogs and then let them go on their way to live the lives they should always have been living.

After a couple of hours, the walk came to an end. We sat and refreshed ourselves with tea and cakes before everyone said their warm farewells and headed off home. The day had been an amazing success and there was not a person or dog present who had not enjoyed themselves. To see Janet and Donna reunited with their foster dogs was enchanting and very special. Without their love and care and the work they do to get the dogs ready for living in normal homes, many would never successfully make the transition from captivity to their new lives. It is not an easy undertaking to take on the responsibility for dogs as hurt and traumatised as puppy farm survivors are, but fosterers do it time and again. At the log seat, Patti had climbed up and sat on Janet's knee as naturally as she had sat cuddled up with her in her office recuperating from cataract surgery a few weeks beforehand. But come the time to go home at the end of the walk, Patti had happily trotted off with her new, devoted family.

The capacity for dogs to so freely and generously love humans, even after the traumas they suffer at the hands of some, is astounding. Patti hadn't forgotten the love shared whilst with Janet. It had helped seed a greater capacity within her to love, as for all the other brave dogs that day. To see this flourish in dogs who for many years had been kept isolated from this emotion is truly humbling.

CHAPTER THIRTEEN

Tasty Sights

*'History, despite its wrenching pain, cannot be unlived, but
if faced with courage, need not be lived again'*
– 'ON THE PULSE OF MORNING', *MAYA ANGELOU*

Shortly after our reunion walk in the New Forest I had to
take Susie-Belle up to Oxford to see Mr Fraser, her
ophthalmologist. When we brought Susie-Belle to live with
us, we knew that we would be taking on the responsibility for
maintaining her eye health following the cataract surgery that
she had received. This involved continuing eye drops for a
little while and being vigilant in future should any
inflammation or other abnormality arise. In addition to this,
she was diagnosed with keratoconjunctivitis sicca (KCS),
commonly called 'dry eye', which is a chronic inflammatory
disease where normal tear production is reduced. Dry eye
didn't really sound that bad to me when I first came across it,

but it's a nasty condition that is incurable and, left untreated, or unresponsive to the drops used to treat it, causes pain, ulceration and eventual blindness. Needless to say, the dogs afflicted with it in puppy farms won't be getting any treatment and sadly it appears to be a pretty common condition amongst survivors. The suffering they must experience caused by the untreated condition whilst in their cruel confinement must be terrible indeed.

I wanted to find out as much as I could about the condition and to see if there was anything nutritionally that we might be able to do with Susie-Belle to tackle it in addition to the regular veterinary care she would need. It's a condition found in several breeds of dog. Miniature schnauzers are prone to it, as are cocker spaniels, pugs, Yorkshire terriers, Cavalier King Charles spaniels – all popular battery farmed breeds – and what happens is the tear producing glands stop working or they are destroyed. As well as providing moisture and with this, comfort, tears also have a role to play in cleansing the eyes and preventing infection. In KCS lack of moisture causes constant inflammation of the cornea, which can develop into ulcers and scarring. Sadly if it reaches the stage of causing blindness, the changes are irreversible and vision loss is permanent.

I was advised to look out for any unusual signs of redness in Susie-Belle's eyes, her rubbing them or squinting. When KCS is first suspected, owners often go to their vet describing these symptoms, which are very similar to simple conjunctivitis so diagnosis of KCS is done through measuring the tear production with a Schirmer Tear Test. Fortunately, this is a simple procedure where a paper strip is placed below the lower eyelid for a minute and the moisture level from the tears rising up the strip is measured. Readings above 15mm are considered normal, between that and 10mm treatment is needed, and below 10mm matters become concerning. Susie-Belle has shown levels as low as 5mm, which have been very worrying indeed.

There are some known causes of KCS, with the most common involving the dog's immune system, which for some reason sets about destroying the tear producing glands. Other causes are physical damage to the tear glands, some drugs and certain infections such as distemper. Unfortunately for some dogs it's a congenital condition and they are born with faulty glands, whilst for others certain hormonal diseases – for example, hypothyroidism – will be the culprit. There are also cases where no identifiable cause is found. Once established, the condition is life-long and requires ongoing treatment. We don't know the reason for Susie-Belle's KCS but with her poor start in life, horrendous hormonal challenges through multiple pregnancies and the terrible life she led, any or all of this could have caused it. What matters for her now is that it is treated and controlled and she never has to suffer again.

She came home to us with the most commonly used treatment for KCS, expensive eye drops that work by decreasing the immune response attacking the tear glands. The majority of dogs on the drops respond well and this treats the disease, although it doesn't cure it so the drops must be continued for life. The drops are easily administered with a dog like Susie-Belle, who is so gentle and compliant and doesn't object to being handled. I dread to think how hard it must be for owners to put eye drops in twice a day with dogs who are terrified of being handled, like so many puppy farm dogs are. A dog like Darcie would go through repeated trauma and the stress for her and her family would not be easy to cope with. I am eternally thankful we have never had any difficulty with Susie-Belle accepting the treatment. Her willingness and courage to accept all we have to do to keep her well has certainly made caring for her a much easier process than it might otherwise have been.

After being home with us for a few weeks, we needed to assess Susie-Belle's degree of response to the eye drops and to get a final signing off from Mr Fraser for her cataract surgery and so it was early October 2011 when we set off to Oxford to see the man who had restored Susie-Belle's eyesight. Meeting Mr Fraser for the first time in his small, friendly Oxfordshire practice, I was immediately aware that here was a man who really loves his work. Originally from Edinburgh, he has performed many cataract operations on Janet's numerous foster dogs. We had a candid chat about the puppy farming industry and the legacy of eye problems that he was seeing in his practice through his connections with Janet and the Diana Brimblecombe Animal Rescue Centre. He ran me through the surgery that Susie-Belle had received earlier in the year, carefully explained what was happening with the KCS and by the time he got to measure her tear production, I felt as if I had known him for a very long while. I always need to get along with my vets and I liked Mr Fraser's frankness and his sensitivity towards Susie-Belle, who was lying on his table in her typically hunched, tight, head down position.

Unfortunately the news on her eyes wasn't good: she did not appear to be responding to the eye drops as the KCS had deteriorated further. Mr Fraser explained that although the majority of dogs do respond to the treatment she was on, in a few cases an alternative approach is needed. A cream normally used for inflammatory skin diseases like eczema had shown benefit in veterinary KCS cases and this was what he proposed we tried next. If Susie-Belle failed to respond, the final option would be to transplant her salivary glands to her eyes to provide lubrication. To me this sounded most alarming, particularly when he went on to explain that the salivary glands would respond in the eyes as they do in the mouth, so anything that caused her to salivate – a tasty meal, for example – would make her eyes run with saliva. This presented a far from appealing future for our little foodie, who loved nothing more than the smells from the kitchen. I sincerely hoped that the new cream would succeed in getting the KCS under control and that I would not be faced with having to make a decision on whether to go down that particular surgical route in future.

Before I left, Mr Fraser gave me clear instructions and a comprehensive demonstration on how to get the cream into Susie-Belle's eyes. I was to retract her upper eyelid firmly, squeeze a small amount of cream underneath the lid and to do so twice daily. There was to be no messing around and not getting it where it was needed, no skipping applications, no doing it any way other than as Mr Fraser showed me. I had my instructions and I was clear on what he expected of me. It was a lot more fiddly and awkward to manage than the eye-specific drops that I had been using, but I assured him that I would soon get the hang of it and be diligent in administering it. I really wanted this to work to avoid having to think about Susie-Belle's eyes being lubricated with saliva every time she ate. For a dog that loved eating in the way she did, amidst a family of foodies, thinking about that alone was enough for me to know that there was no way I would fail to get the cream into her eyes.

The first few times we tried it at home, Susie-Belle was brilliant – patient and tolerant of my cack-handed efforts. I managed to get more greasy cream smeared over her eyebrows than under her eyelid, but after a few messy attempts, I had mastered the technique. Soon she and I were up and away with her new treatment. We quickly established a ritual of applying the cream, followed by a celebratory kiss on her forehead once done, warm with relief that yet another dose had been successfully applied. With each relief-filled kiss I willed the cream to win the battle against her dry eye. The more I thought about the salivary gland transplant option, the more peculiar it seemed and the less likely I felt that I would be able to agree to it. But then what would I do if her eyes began to ulcerate, if the new approach didn't work? I couldn't possibly leave her untreated if there was a surgical option, however odd it seemed. But for Susie-Belle, the smells of food are a regular delight and no doubt provoke healthy salivation in the mouth where intended, this running down her face would be a mighty inconvenience for a dog so attuned to seek out food.

Her food appreciation was growing to be a major part of her personality and whilst we adored feeding her all the good, perfectly balanced meals we did, we also had to watch to make sure she wasn't able to help herself to food she shouldn't have. At times she was more akin to a Labrador than a miniature schnauzer – she was so keen on gobbling up all she was fed, plus more if she could. One memorable day she managed to eat her way through a hefty portion of freshly made chicken fricassée that Michel had unthinkingly left to cool on a stool whilst he lay down on the sofa for a snooze. As I walked in on the scene, there was Susie-Belle with her face in the pot, snout deeply buried in creamy fricassée, Renae alongside her trying to get a taste for herself before her sister finished it all. They were both so intent on their happy gorging that they didn't even look up as I entered the room. As I let out a shocked screech their startled faces turned to me, looking for all the world as if they'd been swimming in fricassée as the garlic and white wine flavoured cream slicked back their eyebrows and dripped from their beards.

Quite how Michel had managed to sleep through the slurping of two dogs devouring their lucky find I couldn't imagine. By the time of discovery, Susie-Belle's tummy was full to bursting point, tight and fat. With its pendulous, over-large nipples her fricasée-filled belly that afternoon resembled a rubber glove that has been blown up with air. I was very worried about her as the dish was full of things she should not have eaten – cream, onions, white wine – and I knew that this could make her very sick. Remarkably, as she settled her heavy, contented body down on her bed, she seemed perfectly fine. All night I watched for signs of illness, only for her to wake the next morning having suffered absolutely no ill effects from her moment of stolen indulgence. We were lucky – she could have been very ill and, from then on, we were far more vigilant about leaving any food within reach of our greedy girl.

If the fricassée incident had occurred after a salivary transplant operation I could imagine her face running uncontrollably with saliva, not a pretty image to ponder. Mr Fraser had warned that he had had to reverse a few cases as the running eyes became too unbearable for the dogs involved. I really didn't want to put Susie-Belle through any surgery unless it was really the only remaining option to preserve her sight. Already she had suffered so much in her life and I had promised her that I would never allow her to suffer again. I diligently continued applying the cream with a good dose of hope and positive thinking with every application and pushed any thoughts of her face running with saliva far from my mind.

At the same time as switching to the new cream, I read about a study that had shown positive results in KCS cases involving the oral intake of the polyunsaturated fatty acids linoleic acid and gamma-linolenic acid (GLA), an omega-6 fatty acid found mainly in plant and seed oils. A healthy canine diet contains both omega-3 and omega-6 essential fatty acids (EFAs) and a correct balance helps reduce inflammation, hence the positive results found in the studies showing significant changes in the inflammation associated with KCS. Although my knowledge of EFAs in human health is reasonably sound, there are differences in canine nutrition and before embarking on supplementing Susie-Belle's diet with EFAs, I wanted to be certain that it was going to be appropriate seeing as she ate an already balanced and varied diet. After further research and inquiry, I found an excellent veterinary-specific EFA supplement and began including it in her daily diet at therapeutic dosage. I didn't expect swift results, but I was hopeful that over time there would be a positive impact on her eye health. But even if that was limited – seeing as EFAs are important for skin and fur – it could only be good for her.

Although dogs bred responsibly can certainly suffer from KCS, it appears that the horrific conditions that puppy farming involves cause endless unnecessary suffering in countless animals that go untreated. Now I know more about the condition, I feel that in view of the situations in which the dogs live and breed this must contribute to causing it. I've come across so many ex-breeders suffering with KCS that there has to be a link. In Susie-Belle's case, she was afflicted by two sight-threatening conditions, cataracts and KCS, and we can only guess how much pain she had suffered and confusion she felt as her vision failed, before she reached the safety of the outside world and proper veterinary care. However, thousands of dogs are not so fortunate. Within months of Susie-Belle leaving her, Janet took in a dog with yet another terrible eye disease that would one day blind her and for which there is no available treatment.

Tica, a petite, black miniature schnauzer, arrived at Janet's in what can only be described as a truly shocking state of neglect, having been taken out of a puppy farm by her rescuers. Janet told me that just when she thinks she has seen the worst case, sadly worse come along and at that time, Tica was by far the worst case. She was gripped by such a dreadful fear of humans that Janet couldn't get near her without Tica backing away and rearing up on her back legs against the wall in terror. It took weeks of patient, tender care to reach a point where Tica would at least allow Janet to approach and get a harness and lead on her so that she could start to explore the outside world.

Even in such highly experienced hands as she was with Janet, it took a long time to coax Tica to a point of being able to relate to humans in ways other than complete distress. Eventually being surrounded by much love and endless patience, Tica did begin to live an almost normal life being fostered by Janet. Then, just as she was almost ready to be placed up for adoption into her forever home, should one come along, Janet began to notice that at dusk Tica seemed unsure of where she was and would bump into things in poor light. She duly took her along to Mr Fraser, suspecting problems with her eyesight. He gave her the crushing news that Tica had PRA (Progressive Retinal Atrophy) and she was slowly losing her vision. Worse still, there was no treatment available. This was truly heartbreaking news for little Tica, who had made courageous progress towards living a normal life. Now she faced yet another cruel challenge.

I felt so sad for Janet when I heard the news, for she had helped so many other dogs to regain their sight following cataract surgery, including my beloved Susie-Belle. To know how much she had grown to love Tica and the tremendous effort that had been involved in getting her to the stage she was at made the news just too painful to grasp. Janet made the unhesitating decision to adopt Tica herself so that she could keep her safe forever and do whatever was needed to adapt her home environment as the dog's vision faded. Although she was terribly upset by the news, there was nothing that anyone could offer that would make it any easier. There is no treatment available for PRA, no magic way to prevent Tica from losing her sight. Ultimately she will go blind and, although many dogs can live well without sight, it is a wicked dose of bad luck that a dog who had to battle so hard to get to a stage of living relatively free of fear should be faced with the confusion of creeping blindness.

But the tentacles of misery of Tica's diagnosis reach far beyond her own life as all the puppies that she was forced to breed in the puppy factory are also at risk of losing their sight, for PRA is an inherited condition. Whilst reputable breeders will screen their dogs and will not breed from them if PRA is found, other, unscrupulous breeders will perform none of these checks. Since PRA is unlikely to show until the dog is around four years or older, they know full well that they are unlikely ever to hear from the owners of those affected. Whilst Tica will be safe with Janet in her loving and secure home and I am certain she will cope well with the challenges that lay ahead, this may not be the case for her many puppies in the years to come. It is likely that she bred tens and tens of puppies during her years as a breeding machine; puppies that will have been sold through online ads, dealers, pet shops and to those who either don't know any better in terms of buying a healthy puppy, or just don't care. When I think about Tica and her darkening world, I hope that her babies are all in safe and loving homes as puppy farming continues to spread suffering far and wide.

CHAPTER FOURTEEN

Sunday in the City

'Twenty years from now you will be more disappointed by the things you didn't do than by the ones you did do. So throw off the bowlines. Sail away from the safe harbor. Catch the trade winds in your sails. Explore. Dream.

Discover' – MARK TWAIN

Whilst we wanted to help Susie-Belle feel secure by keeping to regular routines, we were not going to restrict her to a life of routine and boredom. There had been enough of that in her past. All the routines in her life up to this point had been unpleasant, centred round cycles of enforced mating, pregnancy and birth. What we wanted for her now was a daily life filled with novelty for novelty equals excitement for dogs. Yes, she needed routine, but more than that she needed stimulation. We wanted to show her that life is not boring and each day should be lived, not endured. And we wanted to share with her our own enjoyment in finding new places to explore. You don't have to be an expert in dog psychology to recognise that normal dogs perk up when we take them to places they have never been to before, or been away from for some time. As they rush around off-lead, taking in the new air flush with exciting smells, all their senses alive and alert, no one could argue that happy dogs have any problems experiencing new things.

Dogs thrive when their senses are stimulated. In Susie-Belle's case we had already seen how linked her olfactory and taste senses were to her state of mind. Any whiff of something cooking and she came out of her shell and started to engage with us. Dogs seem able to sleep through noise and Susie-Belle was no exception, but where sound may disturb dozing humans, smell seems to have the same effect on dogs. She could be apparently fast asleep one second and on full kitchen alert the next, should she catch the scent of cooking. So we knew that her senses worked perfectly and hoped that a rich assortment of activity outside the home would steadily bring her increasing happiness. If she had plenty of things to sense all around we hoped this would help her to blossom into the happy dog we were convinced she could be. Although she was still very timid we were seeing enough signs to suggest there was a normal dog there, one that could be happy. Although only time would tell whether her previous life had trapped her in a perpetual state of timidity what was needed was suitable encouragement and plenty of opportunity for the true Susie-Belle to emerge when ready, we felt.

Dogs are naturally curious creatures. I wanted to tap into Susie-Belle's natural inquisitiveness, even if she didn't yet know that this was a possible state of being. For dogs whose lives are confined to small concrete pens or wire cages, their capacity for enjoyable, unfettered curiosity is severely curtailed. But I could see no good reason why this natural behaviour should not be encouraged in Susie-Belle now that she was safely living with us. Thinking how animated dogs are when they are somewhere new, how they hurtle around fizzing with excitement, I wanted at the very least to offer our special dog the chance to experience some of this and if my instincts were right, move into a happy state of being. So we decided to do something completely different to what she had so far experienced and travel with her to London one Sunday morning to take part in a group dog walk in Hyde Park.

Neither Michel nor I are great fans of spending time in cities and usually do all we can to avoid going to London despite living within easy reach of the capital. But in the spirit of sharing new experiences with Susie-Belle, we agreed that to stretch ourselves and get out of our usual comfort zone of country walks would be as good for us as for her. The plan was to meet everyone in Hyde Park late morning and amble round together for a couple of hours, letting the dogs enjoy the freedom of being in one of London's largest open spaces. The park covers 350 acres and is a popular place for Londoners, tourists and visitors alike. I was a little anxious about how Susie-Belle would fare if it was busy but as it was November I hoped the number of visitors would be manageable.

We have several options for getting to London from where we live and I considered each one in the days leading up to the walk. Our friend Dean was taking his dog, Rupert, who was similar in age to Renae, by train and underground Tube, having done so a couple of times during the summer. Rupert had taken to travelling by train with absolutely no problems and seeing Dean's photographs of him sitting on the Tube looking calm and confident, I fleetingly wondered whether this might be an adventure we could share with our girls. In the end, my own nerves at taking both Renae and Susie-Belle on public transport got the better of me and we made it into the centre of London the easy way: by car. Being early on a Sunday morning the drive in was quiet and we managed to find a parking spot within a short walking distance of Hyde Park itself. It couldn't have been an easier introduction to the delights of the big city for our puppy farm girl.

Walking Susie-Belle along the London pavements was a novelty for me as much as for her. I had never walked a dog in a city environment before and although I know millions of owners and dogs do so every day, I was surprised how exciting it was for me, let alone my dogs. Although the roads were not manically busy, the traffic was starting to build up and the noise level increased but the buzz of activity seemed energising rather than alarming, both for Susie-Belle and me. There were continuous sounds, a lot of it in the background, but every few minutes something sharper – a car alarm in a side street, the siren of an emergency vehicle – and as we reached the main roads, the thundering noise of buses as they trundled past. Even on a Sunday morning activity was constant in the capital, with people suddenly appearing from doorways and hurrying past, a guy sweeping rubbish from his shop front, pushing it into the road across our path, oblivious to us being there. Susie-Belle trotted alongside me with no signs of being stressed and as I looked down at her, I marvelled at how far removed she was that morning in the streets of London from the broken dog she had been a few months earlier when she left the prison life from which she'd been rescued behind. As Renae stopped to sniff a novel London pavement smell, Susie-Belle trotted to catch her up and share in the aromatic pleasure and in this stop, sniff, start fashion we eventually crossed the busy Kensington Road and made our way into Hyde Park. We joined the growing group of dogs waiting by the meeting point, a large number of them schnauzers. I don't know about Susie-Belle, but I was glad to leave the noise of the streets behind and enter the relative haven of the park. Not that it was quiet, but it was certainly calmer.

There were some people and dogs that we had met before on walks but many new faces had made it to the city that morning to join in. With a choice of ways to access London, people had travelled good distances to take part and it was one of the largest group walks we had done to date. Several had come by public transport and crossed London by Tube and bus. Though impressed by their intrepidity, I knew that we had made the right decision with Renae and Susie-Belle to use the car. I didn't have the confidence to take them on the Tube and if I didn't feel confident, it would hopelessly affect their experience. Right now, they were both happy to be amongst friends, old and new, and didn't care how they had got there. Of course they didn't even care that they were in London – they were somewhere new and exciting, that's what was important to them.

A normal, happy dog's default behaviour is friendly, to meet and greet another dog or human with a natural enthusiasm that other animals don't tend to show. Cats are often wary on meeting each other but dogs with healthy social skills want to make friends and extend this to humans. As we stood in Hyde Park these normal canine greetings were fully on show and it was reassuring to see Susie-Belle move forward to interact with the dogs around her. Although she kept looking over her shoulder whenever she sensed any human getting too close for comfort, her eagerness to meet the dogs neutralised any anxiety she might have felt about the humans attached to them. This was a big improvement from her first trip out to Norbury Park at the start of the summer when her eyes had flashed full of fear every time a person had come too close and she had hung to the back of the group, head low, shoulders down. I relaxed, knowing she was feeling good about being where she was right at that moment, and felt proud of my brave girl for making her sweet progress through our life together so far.

Once the group had assembled we set off in the direction of the Serpentine Lake, where those who wished could get refreshments before heading back. I was surprised to find the park as busy as it was – the late autumn sun had clearly brought many people out for a Sunday walk. As we sauntered along, taking our time and enjoying the moment, the high number of schnauzers in the group attracted a lot of attention from onlookers. Most passers-by seemed amused to see so many congregating and many shared pleasantries as we walked through the park. Being London, amusing sights are nothing unusual so it was funny to see astonishment on the faces of some as they saw one, then another, and another and yet another schnauzer streaming along, running and bounding to keep up with the friendly canine crowd. There were also the not amused, the ones who pretended not to notice the exuberance of dogs enjoying the park that sunny Sunday, keeping their noses in the air and their faces fixed. I pitied those who could not take even the smallest pleasure in seeing the natural warmth and joy on display all around them. To see the dogs running happily, freely together in the middle of the capital city, was priceless entertainment and brought a lot of happiness for many strangers that day.

Once we had set off walking, Susie-Belle took her customary place behind my heels and although off-lead and in theory she was able to wander at will, she chose to stay close. Occasionally she would venture slightly to the side if a particularly enticing aroma caught her attention, but swiftly take up her original position if I continued to walk on. For much of the walk she was glued to my feet. Many owners would be delighted to have a dog do such a faultless demonstration of heel walking in a busy, distracting location, but I longed for the day that Susie-Belle would feel secure enough to leave my side. Then I would know for sure that she had let go of her fears. Although she seemed happy in the company of the dogs, once we were walking she wouldn't freely mingle with them. Her ingrained anxiety about having anyone behind her meant that if she started to pull ahead of my feet at any stage, as soon as she realised this she would stop, look over both shoulders and wait for people to pass. Once she felt she was at the back of the crowd of feet, she continued trotting along. For much of the time I lingered at the back of the group to keep her happy and safe. However, because of the volume of people out walking and the constant movement all around, it was impossible to stay at the back for long as people soon came up behind us.

As we continued through the park, I focussed on keeping Susie-Belle content and watched out for signs of her being stressed or overwhelmed. However, she was fine and soon seemed happily immersed in the buzz of the walk. At times we became momentarily separated and as I scanned the throng of feet I would see her trotting ahead, nose down, stuck close to the heels of strangers who were oblivious to the quiet little dog following them. As I called her back, or ran up to get her attention, I realised that she didn't much care whose feet she was following. I found this saddening and wondered if this reflected a lack of attachment to us, to me. Was she not able to feel part of our group, our family yet? Should I worry that one set of human feet seemed pretty much the same to her? Now, I realise at that point she had spent longer with Janet than us and so maybe she wasn't yet able, or quite ready to bond with us. Hard as it is for me to think this, whilst she held a central place in my heart at that stage in her life with us, for Susie-Belle we may just have been another set of humans with whom she was sharing space. True we were people who cared for her, provided food, shelter, warmth and love, but so had Janet, in all likelihood the first kind and compassionate human that Susie-Belle would have spent any time with.

But then, just as Susie-Belle had really begun to settle into Janet's life and started to show her true personality, she had been whisked away and had to begin all over again in a strange home with a new set of humans. Having left Janet behind, how could she possibly know that the same wasn't going to happen again? She had once been brave and allowed herself to trust Janet, could she risk doing so again with us? If Mr Coode, the homeopathic vet, was right and loss, sadness, bereavement and grief affected a large part of Susie-Belle's psyche, it would take a while yet for her to trust again. Following that day in Hyde Park, I thought a lot about how readily she had attached herself to the feet of strangers and it was a salutary reminder for me that the unimaginable emotional challenges that she had gone through in her life hadn't ended when she left the puppy farm or even when she joined our home. By taking her away from Janet, although in the long term this would provide her with the best life possible, she didn't of course know that.

Although I would like to think she could feel and understand we loved her deeply, she was more than likely not going to allow herself to love or trust us for a good long while. Just because we knew that we would never leave her, she herself didn't have that knowledge. We had to be aware that Susie-Belle would need a long time yet before she could properly trust us, to relax fully into our home and feel that it was as much hers as ours. To trust that we would never abandon or take her away; to know that she was with us for the rest of her life. I believe that this must be common amongst all rescue dogs, not only those who survive the horrific battery farming business. Where dogs from those backgrounds have additional problems to contend with, dogs that live one day in homes as pets and do know human kindness but then for whatever reason on another day are surrendered to shelters, or just dumped, the break of trust they experience must be tremendous. To recover from that and for them ever to regain trust in humans again is a remarkable feat of courage in my opinion.

We eventually arrived at the Serpentine Lake and as we neared the café area, the crowds were steadily growing and the number of people milling around became a little too much for us. In fact we had stumbled upon a huge Christmas attraction, the Hyde Park Winter Wonderland. No wonder the crowds were big – there was a large, busy Christmas market and fun fair with ice rink, shopping and festive attractions. People were everywhere, cooking smells floated on the air, laughter and chatter filled our ears along with the harsh artificial sounds of the fun fair; we strained to hear one another speak. The atmosphere was frenetic, the noise incredible and even to me, let alone Susie-Belle, a touch overwhelming. This was definitely too much for her and us so we called it a day. It had been a successful trip out, she had coped very well with the challenge of London and a large busy park and we didn't want to spoil it by undoing any good progress that may have been achieved that day.

We said our goodbyes and headed back through the park towards the quiet safety of the car. There were fewer people around than when we had passed through earlier and I watched with warm satisfaction as Susie-Belle tottered along with Renae, who by now was staying closer to her side as she didn't have her friends to run with. As we stood and took a photograph of them standing together with the Royal Albert Hall as backdrop, I tried hard to imagine what must be going through their minds. For Renae, I thought it would be pretty simple – she had enjoyed a day out with her friends, run around chasing squirrels, hurtled through piles of fallen leaves and most likely wondered now where everyone had gone. But for Susie-Belle the thoughts might run deeper. Whilst she may have been relieved it was all over, I like to think internally she was fizzing with new sensory experiences, new memories to rub out some of the bad.

That afternoon in the creeping early winter chill as we crossed Hyde Park I knew deep in my heart that our decision to bring Susie-Belle out to play that day had been completely right. I knew she could thrive in novel places, so long as we looked out for her, understood her limitations and acted to give her peace, quiet and familiarity when that was what she needed.

CHAPTER FIFTEEN

Susie-Belle Arrives in France

'We delight in the beauty of the butterfly, but rarely admit the changes it has gone through to achieve that beauty' –

MAYA ANGELOU

Our first trip to France with Susie-Belle came at Christmas, four months after she had been with us. By that time we were beginning to get to know her personality better and she was blossoming in so many ways. When we were in our familiar places walking she was starting to potter alongside Renae more and more rather than sticking to our heels. She would enjoy her morning sniffing and peeing round the park, checking what had changed from the previous night's smells and adding her own contributions. She was interacting well with all the dogs we met and people were remarking on how well she seemed to be settling in. There remained plenty of issues with nervousness in new environments and when strangers approached she would still hang her head, cast her eyes down and shrink away if she could. But we were still delighted with how well she was developing and small, subtle things we saw daily showed us she was feeling less anxious and more relaxed in her own self.

I noticed her eyes appeared bigger, softer, more rounded and it wasn't until I sensed this faintest of changes that I realised they had been held tight and small with muscle tension and stress. Signs like this only Michel and I noticed as we were attuned to her in ways others couldn't be and to a casual observer her eyes would just have been the eyes of a dog. How something so subtle could reveal so much about Susie-Belle's inner self was truly enlightening. Although we knew we could never undo her past, it was deeply pleasing to know that we were helping her to move on and let go of it. I wanted to believe that one day, memories of those who had imprisoned and abused her for years would leave her mind forever if we kept carrying her forwards and filling her life with love and joy. My deepest hope was that the hurt and pain that she had gone through for so many years would be fully healed and permanently forgotten if we found the right ways to help her.

Having France in December to plan ahead for did focus my mind on ensuring Susie-Belle was given every opportunity to stretch herself and I planned plenty of mini challenges to help her become the dog I knew she could be. Of most importance in terms of her being happy with what would be regular trips across the Channel was her ability to travel in the car for long periods. The journey is one that we do every few weeks throughout the year and involves around twelve hours in the car. Renae has never had a problem in the car – she sits for long spells with her nose up against the glass, content to watch the world fly past as we motor along. As soon as Susie-Belle arrived, we got into habits of regular car trips and thankfully she settled into these without any sign of distress so I was hopeful she would follow Renae's lead as she had in so many other ways and embrace the mid-winter drive as one of her positive new experiences. Christmas came and went at home in England and as soon as we could, we packed up the house and loaded the car, setting off in the early hours to head down to the Channel and get on our way.

The winter drives are always a little more demanding, involving longer hours of darkness and unpredictable weather conditions, but on this one, as the sun came up and we sped south, the day promised to be a bright, cold and clear one to travel on. Being aware of Susie-Belle's way of never complaining or letting us know if she was in need of anything, we made a few extra stops than we normally do to pre-empt any problems she might have. Her self-contained manner was one that must have helped her get through the years of loneliness and torture in the battery farm but now we were there to help with anything she needed, only she didn't yet know this, or realise she could profit from our willingness to do all we could for her. A few weeks after our trip to France, I massaged her legs and checked her feet only to find she was missing a whole claw. It looked as though it had been recently lost and our vet agreed, saying she thought it had been ripped out, probably by being caught on something.

Susie-Belle had shown no sign of being in pain, yet she must have been as the claw had gone completely. Her stoicism was impressive, but sad – the thought of her suffering at all, ever again in her life, was something that deeply upset me. I hoped that when she came to live with us never again would she have to experience pain and I would do all I could to protect her from any suffering. I wanted her to know that she could seek comfort and help whenever she needed or wanted it, but it would be a long time for this to happen – she was after all drawing on a lifetime of survival and self-sufficiency.

As we headed down through France, we were excited about it being her first trip but of course she had no idea she was anywhere other than just down the road out on a regular car ride, albeit a long one. The incongruity of a puppy farm survivor turfed out of a barn in a state of shocking neglect now ending the year holidaying in France warmed our hearts. Whilst we stood shivering in the winter air, on a grass verge somewhere in the Loire Valley, she painstakingly finished her appraisal of the roadside aromas, behaving all the while like a perfectly happy dog, one whose emotional scars were certainly fading. Susie-Belle's life may have nearly ended in a puppy farm and those who confined her almost succeeded in breaking her spirit, but looking at her then, I was struck by how her broken body and damaged mind were now well on the way to being whole again. How I would have liked those who abused her until they wore her almost to death to see her now; to poke them in the eye with her rising strength and courage and to reveal the darkness of their inhumanity through the light of her survivorship. Susie-Belle's happy soul was singing loud and clear to me that cold day in December somewhere in la belle France and mine responded in kind; I was profoundly happy knowing she was firmly on the road to being a very contented little dog for the first time in her life in spite of the suffering she had survived.

Our house is located in the southwest of France, in a perfect region for a family of foodies: the Perigord, or as the British know it better, the Dordogne, which is renowned for its cuisine. We were sure that Susie-Belle would thrive during her time there, not only because of culinary indulgence, but also because it is such a peaceful and pleasant place. It's a popular destination for holidaymakers visiting the region in summer to enjoy temperatures not far off Mediterranean norms. For us it's common to doze away August afternoons in the cool of the shuttered house, waiting for the blistering heat to subside before we venture into the shade of the garden to spend a balmy evening under the stars. The summer heat can be intense but for the majority of the time we are there it tends to be pleasant rather than oppressive. Over the years many an afternoon was spent with Jasmine cooling her paws in the river at the bottom of our hill on warm days. We looked forward to sharing the pleasure with Susie-Belle but on that first visit in mid-winter this was the last thing on our minds.

The weather had been very cold before we arrived with a light snowfall a few days beforehand so we arrived to an icy, frozen vista. We don't get much snow but temperatures can fall well below freezing and we often wake on winter mornings to find the landscape thick with crisp, sparkling frost. We are deep in the rural countryside and unlike where we live in the UK where we feel eternally squeezed into smaller and noisier spaces, in France we are surrounded by fields, forests and open space – and lots of it. Our house stands on a hill and looks out over a bucolic valley, through which the River Dronne runs. On autumn mornings we open the shutters to some of our favourite views of the valley cloaked in light mist rising from the river, with the trees pushing up through it. But on winter mornings all is clear, the trees are stripped of their foliage and we can see for miles out across the valley. Way over on the other side, the village that disappears amidst the thick curtain of leafy green trees in spring and summer suddenly reappears on our winter visits, distant amber rooftops catching the weak, wintry sun.

Looking out up along the lane leading from the house, there are acres of fields which in summer are splashed with the yellow and gold of sunflowers and corn. There are pockets of pine forest and mixed woodland dotting the landscape, which provide welcome shade on our summer walks.

Arriving at the house in the early dusk of winter, the clear sky promised a cold night ahead. We let Susie-Belle explore her surroundings whilst Renae went straight to visit all her familiar spots in the garden and up the lane. Both had travelled well with no sign of any problem with either of them; Renae we had known would be fine and with her confident sister at her side, helping her on levels we will never properly understand, Susie-Belle had done the same. After a brief check of the exterior, they were happy to settle indoors as we unloaded the car, lit the fire and settled in for the night. We'd brought the Christmas leftovers with us and supper for everyone involved various tastes of turkey. For us it was the inevitable cold meat platter with chutneys and the girls enjoyed chopped turkey giblets with a healthy dollop of goat's yoghurt. We headed off to bed early with full tummies, happy but weary from the long day spent travelling.

Although I enjoy the peaceful, warm summers we spend in France, I really cherish the additional serenity and bare beauty of the winter countryside. The roads and lanes are silent, villages appear dormant and we can go for days and see no one. Where we are, even in the height of the summer there are never a lot of people around, but in December and January when the cold keeps people tucked away indoors there are fewer still. I knew Susie-Belle would benefit from the tranquillity we find in France and our first few days were cold, bright and dry. We walked for miles in the peace of the winter landscape, letting her settle into the new environment.

Since being with us, we had steadily been increasing the distances that we walked with her, gradually building her fitness. By December she could comfortably keep pace with us over a reasonable distance and without the nagging noise and unpredictability of traffic and people on pavements to worry her, she relaxed more and more on every walk. Each time she accompanied us, nose close to the ground taking in all the new country smells, her tail-stump twitched like a beacon emitting pure pleasure when something caught her attention. We had already noticed at home that her tail twitches were gradually increasing in frequency and intensity, on holiday they very clearly signalled a daily rise in Susie-Belle's internal pleasure centre.

Sadly the early dry, cold, crisp days soon turned to dreary wet ones and on a few walks we found ourselves getting caught in heavy downpours with nowhere to shelter. Despite being suitably dressed, it's never enjoyable getting home with two wet and cold schnauzers – a breed not renowned for its enjoyment of water. Although some schnauzers are more weatherproof than others, we have yet to live with one who willingly goes out in the rain. Nevertheless we were committed to our walks and once out, unless hit by a truly torrential downpour, neither dog seemed to mind carrying on once their initial mad shaking off of the raindrops subsided. 'The Great-Schnauzer-Shake-Off', as we termed it, would commence the second either of them felt the first spot of moisture fall on them and would involve stopping immediately in their tracks then frantically and with great intent shaking every trace of moisture from themselves, head twirling in reverse direction to the body, which would be lifted free of the ground by the momentum created. It really was a sight to see and would continue every few paw steps until each of them eventually conceded defeat and stretched the time between shakes to a point where we could continue moving on with the walk.

Returning from a chilly walk one morning when we'd been caught in a heavy downpour, we were coming down our lane approaching the house, Renae and Susie-Belle appearing eager to get back into the warm and dry, us talking about a late breakfast and hot showers all round. Just as we rounded the corner ahead of the house, out in the lane one of our neighbour's chickens was wandering, minding it's own business. They are usually confined behind a low hedge and wire fence and Renae had spent the summer seemingly fascinated by them every time we passed by, quietly peering through the fence to observe the flock. On the days Susie-Belle had passed by she preferred to concentrate on keeping her nose down, close to our heels, the usual Susie-Belle walking style in new places that we had grown accustomed to and had shown no interest in the hens at all… until now.

We all saw the stray bird together, Renae calmly trotting up to take a closer inspection. Just as I thought that it would be wise to clip on her lead, the bird sensed danger and began flapping and squawking, at which point Renae's instincts lit up and off she shot, swiftly followed by Susie-Belle. As the chicken panicked and whirled and tried to get back to safety over the hedge, Susie-Belle dashed across the lane to grab it. We had never seen her move so fast and were so taken by surprise at her speed and the ensuing frenzy that we took a second too long to react and she seemed to grab the bird's flapping wing. But, just in the nick of time we came to our senses and as I grabbed a flustered Renae and intense, wriggling Susie-Belle, Michel rescued the bird, which had lodged itself deep in the prickly hedge. Luckily it wasn't injured despite all its noise and flustering, and as Michel dropped it over the hedge it ran over fast to join the safety of the rest of the flock.

I was pleased no harm had been done. I would have been upset, and embarrassed to tell the neighbour that one of his chickens had been injured or killed. But a tiny part of me was also glad that Susie-Belle had normal schnauzer instincts and reflexes that, despite her oppressed life, these days were sharp enough to see a chance opportunity for catching some prey. Schnauzers do have a healthy prey drive, some stronger than others. Jasmine was a keen chaser of anything that she thought she might catch, but we had not seen it yet in either Renae or Susie-Belle. Although not a behaviour that we particularly want to encourage in our dogs, it was heartening, if slightly shocking, to see the normal dog rise to the fore in Susie-Belle that morning.

We were joined for New Year by my brother and his family and decided to celebrate New Year's Eve at home with a French culinary feast. Michel spent the day preparing and cooking a menu suitably Gallic in style. We ate quails with a champagne and grape sauce, preceded by one of the most typically French dishes, *cuisses de grenouille*. We had decided to have frogs' legs as a bit of fun for my young niece and nephew, not really expecting them to be enjoyed – a predictable British aversion to the French culinary classic being alive and well in my family. As the children squirmed and face-pulled at the thought of their starter, we assured them that they would be just like chicken... but not quite. That evening Michel's version of frogs' legs tasted like the best fried chicken imaginable and despite their initial reluctance, once they started on them the children devoured the plateful that was served and looked for more.

And it wasn't only the children who enjoyed some frogs' legs that holiday. We tentatively examined them raw and decided there was no good reason why our raw-fed dogs shouldn't try them. Susie-Belle tucked in with predictable enthusiasm, crunching through the soft bones without hesitation. Renae was less sure and took longer to be convinced they were a worthy meal, giving her sister puzzled looks as she picked up, dropped and eventually after much deliberation finally ate the tiny legs whilst Susie-Belle sped through hers. Amphibian starter devoured, we rounded off their celebratory supper with a taster dish of quail for them – seeing as it was New Year's Eve a little indulgence seemed in order.

The rest of the holiday remained cold and wet until the very last day when the sun made a welcome return. As we were travelling the following day this was fortunate as we felt inspired to take the dogs for a decent long walk to exercise them nicely, knowing they would be resting in the car the next day. We headed out to one of our favourite walking places but one that we knew would be muddy after all the rain. Long stretches of the walk cross fields and there are several sections that become waterlogged after heavy rain, but as I planned to bath the dogs that day, it seemed worth the mud we would trek back to the house with.

As we made our way up one of the steepest of the hills, the views stretching out ahead were stunning; the sun reflected off sparkling pools of water that lay in distant fields. After a couple of hours, we headed home and took a turn down a path that we thought was a shortcut. As we descended the path, it became muddier and wetter, with rivulets of rainwater pouring alongside it. When at last we reached the bottom of the track we were met by a flooded brook, spilling across the path and into the surrounding fields. To one side was a narrow wooden bridge half-hidden by brambles and overgrowth. It was clear not many trod this route, especially not in winter. The scramble to the rickety bridge through the brambles seemed far from inviting and we knew Susie-Belle and Renae wouldn't manage it without being carried. As we stood dithering about which way to get through and who was carrying whom, determined as ever, Susie-Belle made her own decision and head down, shoulders spread, started wading into the cold waters of the stream. Luckily the water wasn't deep, reaching only to her belly, but her decisiveness prompted us both to get moving to meet her on the other side. I pushed through the brambles and made my way over the bridge, leaving Michel to scoop up Renae, who showed no willingness to follow her sister into the icy water.

As we headed home, Susie-Belle dripping but none the worse for her cold water dip, I looked ahead to the summer with a renewed optimism that I might have a swimming schnauzer beside me in the warmer rivers and lakes of France.

CHAPTER SIXTEEN

No More Skinny Susie-Belle

'I think… if it is true that there are as many minds as there are heads, then there are as many kinds of love as there are hearts'

— ANNA KARENINA, *LEO TOLSTOY*

Soon after we got back to the UK from our first trip to France with Susie-Belle she was due to visit Mr Fraser in Oxford to see how her eyes were responding to the treatment for her KCS. The cream was awkward to apply and although she was patient with me (and brilliant), in the beginning I wasn't so good. With each application I managed to get a load smeared over her eyebrows for quite a while until I had mastered my technique. But I thought we were now doing well and I was hopeful that her tear production readings would show an improvement, or at least no further deterioration. But the news Mr Fraser gave us was mixed.

The left eye, the one with the new lens and good vision and thus most important, did seem to be responding well to the cream and her readings were above 10mm. However, the right one had deteriorated, with a reading now at 5mm. At this level things become concerning and once again Mr Fraser and I had a conversation about the possibility of moving Susie-Belle's salivary glands to her eyes. But the idea had become no more appealing to me than when he had first mentioned it as a possible therapeutic option and I made the long drive home after our appointment burdened by gloomy thoughts. We had agreed that I would continue with the cream for a further couple of months, adding artificial tears to lubricate her eyes to keep them moist and help further protect her corneas from ulceration.

I had rechecked my cream applying technique with Mr Fraser and although I was doing fine, we both thought that I could do with retracting her eyelids a bit more firmly, allowing more of the cream a chance to stay where it was needed. I hoped that minor tweaks in my technique might make all the difference to her future eye health; all the hope I could hang onto was welcome as visions of her face soaked in saliva haunted me. Also, I revisited some of the research about the possible role that essential fatty acids (EFAs) in her diet might play and decided that in order to give her maximum dietary support I would introduce a good supplement in addition to what I had already been using. My research suggested that for there to be therapeutic effect, variety and the correct dosage would help and I put renewed effort into sourcing the best oils, the best oily-rich foods and giving her the best meals possible for her needs. At this point my menu planning for Susie-Belle became even more focussed and complex – it was the least I could do for my treasured companion.

A few weeks after the visit to Mr Fraser however, I noticed one morning that Susie-Belle was pawing her face and rubbing it along her bed, the sofa and door-frames. Something was clearly uncomfortable and bothering her so I made an appointment at our local vet for later that day. It was a locum on duty as our regular vet was away, so after my usual rather intense instructions about the vital need to treat her carefully, patiently, sensitively – none of which is actually necessary for me to lecture on in our practice as everyone shows these qualities without fail but I can't help myself – I let him give her left eye a thorough inspection. She had an ulcer on her cornea. This was news that I did not want to hear and my heart sank as my mind raced ahead to unbearable images of Susie-Belle having painful surgery, losing her sight; suffering agonies. Somehow I rapidly pulled myself together and listened to what I needed to do for her. The vet explained that although there was an obvious possibility that the ulcer was linked to a deterioration in her KCS and overall eye health, it was just as feasible that she had sustained a minor surface scratch to the eye and that it would heal well with the treatment he was to give and be no more sinister than that. He was very good at managing and reassuring me but I insisted on getting a referral to the local ophthalmologist as I knew that to get up to Oxford to Mr Fraser would be difficult for a few days.

As it happens, the ophthalmologist that I was referred to locally, Mr Jeff Yellowley, has been in practice since 1985 and qualified around the same time as Mr Fraser. Being very particular about which vets I trust to take care of my dogs, and especially so when it comes to Susie-Belle's eyes, I quizzed the nursing staff at my practice about their impression of Mr Yellowley as they make regular referrals to him. I was satisfied enough to at least have an initial consultation. Meeting him the next day I knew that he would take care of Susie-Belle perfectly. He was sweet, gentle and seemed in no rush at all to get through the appointment. A talkative Geordie from the northeast of England, I instantly warmed to him and liked the soothing voice he used to put Susie-Belle at ease, settling her with his undisguised compassion. I talked him through her history and explained the background to her eyes, her current and past treatment and gave him the records from Mr Fraser that I had with me. Mr Yellowley agreed with the locum that the corneal ulceration was superficial and could well have occurred from a minor local abrasion and may be unrelated to the KCS. He gave me some drops to use and urged me to remain positive about the outcome.

A week later we returned to Mr Yellowley and made the formal switch to his practice for Susie-Belle's eyes. In many ways I was sad to leave Mr Fraser's care as he had done her cataract operation and looked after her whilst she had been at her lowest, newly out of the puppy farm, but I had no doubts that she would be in equally good hands now. This time the news was better: her ulcer had healed and the tear production readings were stable, slightly improved from the last recorded at Mr Fraser's. Although I knew I could not read too much into this latest result as they had fluctuated up and down since monitoring had started, I was hopeful just maybe the supplements and dietary focus we were undertaking may be starting to have an effect. We had been noticing that Susie-Belle's overall energy seemed to be improving all the time now and she had days when she seemed to positively glow with health. Her coat was starting to thicken nicely and had a pleasing shine to it.

However, one thing of which we had also guiltily become aware was that her unlimited joy of eating and our eagerness to satisfy her was resulting in a little too much weight gain. There was no trace now of the once skinny Susie-Belle, these days she was softly well rounded, even bordering on plump. Our greedy girl was becoming a little fatty and we had to take full responsibility for it. Much as we loved to see Susie-Belle enjoying her culinary life and showing us every day how much happier she felt, especially when mealtimes arrived, we knew that it would never be the right thing for her health to allow obesity to set in. I knew that the food she was getting was the best she could have, her diet was perfectly balanced nutritionally for her needs but her meals were too big. Whilst I did take care with the fat content, especially in view of the important role of EFAs and the need to get the balance right, what I had been slack in maintaining was correct portion control.

Renae kept an ideal weight, but she ran around a lot more than Susie-Belle, who preferred a somewhat sedate approach to life and her walks. Where Renae would hurtle around, back and forth between us whilst we were out walking, Susie-Belle's style was better described as a gentle plod. She had excellent endurance, and could happily walk with us for some miles, but she was no fat-burning sprinter. On days when she felt a bit more sprightly and confident, she would totter off with Renae for a while only to glance over her shoulder, stop and wait for us to catch up before tucking herself in again beside our feet to continue her ambling pace. She was adept at saving energy and could see little reason to run back to us when she knew we would come to her and she could once again take up her favourite position at our feet. In the house, where she had once lain hunched and tense on her bed with her limbs tucked tightly underneath her, now she would lay relaxed on her side like any normal dog, showing us her plump, contented belly. It was a gorgeous sight and one we jokingly tagged our special 'plumpilicious' belly view but we knew for the good of her health we had to get her back on track and portion control must be tightened up.

Aside from me being a weak pushover at the sight of her beautiful, pleading face gazing up at me whenever she wanted a snack, and Susie-Belle being greedy, another factor in her weight gain was our over-generous use of food as reward. We hadn't done any traditional training with her because it didn't seem fair to make a dog who had survived what she had survived and known no kindness or reward to have to work for it now. Susie-Belle was opening up to us, revealing her true personality through her foodie enjoyment and we embraced this to the max and experimented with tasty homemade treats. However, where Renae always had to do something to be rewarded, Susie-Belle managed to get the same for just being there, for being our own special Susie-Belle. As Renae would fly back across the field at the sound of my whistle to get a tiny piece of Michel's freshly baked cheese biscuits, Susie-Belle would already be at my feet, having not moved far, looking up at me with her big, precious, shining brown eyes. She would get the same, for zero effort. It had to stop if she was to avoid obesity.

Luckily I was in regular contact with Janet, which helped to focus my mind on keeping Susie-Belle's weight under control. I knew that I would have some explaining to do whenever we met up, should I have a little fat dog with me when Janet had entrusted her into my care. I did take heart, however, from a story Janet told me about Susie-Belle's time with her, where she was already showing early signs of impressive manipulative skills when it came to getting herself some treats.

*You could see early on what a loving character she had;
she was always so sweet – if not a bit cheeky at times. I
shall never forget the day she was in our front paddock
with my dogs, including Monkey. The gate at the top of
the paddock that leads into the sheep compound wasn't
very secure and the dogs would sometimes break through
to sample the sheep poo. We had a box of treats in the
paddock which we would rattle to get Monkey back when
she was up there as she was particularly obsessed with
sheep poo. One day Susie-Belle realised the quickest way
to get the treats was to go straight up to the gate and stand
there, knowing we would rattle the treats to get her back.
She kept doing this over and over, every day. We could all
see that she didn't really want the sheep poo at all – it was
just her cheeky way of getting herself some treats. It made
us all laugh every time. She had the best recall ever in
that paddock!*

It was mildly reassuring to know that I was not alone in having
ridiculously low levels of willpower when it came to saying no
to Susie-Belle and her belly. Dogs have a knack of being
directly able to tap into our resistance: they express emotions
so openly, so freely. And Susie-Belle's hard life had well
prepared her to perform a superbly intense expression of
serious hunger, of near starvation, should she not get that
teeny last piece of liver cake poorly hidden in my hand.
Resisting her seductive face was a hard challenge, especially as
I myself enjoy food so much and fully empathised with her.
Everyone in our household loves their food – it's a home rich
with food enjoyment – but we had to take proper
responsibility for Susie-Belle and recognise that we should
know best what was good for her, however intently she stared

at me and tried to persuade otherwise. Some tough love was needed to rectify the creeping weight gain before it became less amusing. I knew I had to stiffen my resolve and so I got us a set of weighing scales.

CHAPTER SEVENTEEN

Up and Down

'I see at intervals the glance of a curious sort of bird through the close-set bars of a cage: a vivid, restless, resolute captive is there; were it but free, it would soar cloud-high'
– JANE EYRE, *CHARLOTTE BRONTE*

As well as Susie-Belle's reduction in calorie intake, we were steadily building up her fitness through longer, regular walks. By the spring she was looking great, moving in a much more relaxed way and even beginning to keep up with Renae at times as they pootled round the fields each day. Seeing her move away from our feet and saunter over to other dogs, or join Renae in checking out some fascinating smell made us smile every time. It was a real sign that she felt more at ease and confident enough to be away from us, even if it was by only a short distance and time. Her increased activity and lower level of food intake soon started to deal with the excess

161

weight she had accumulated through the winter and she began to regain a waistline.

Being Susie-Belle it had not been difficult to find a whole range of low-fat treats to keep her happy as she is so easy to please and greedy for anything. We had introduced a variety of dried fish treats, which are low fat, stink the house out but provide a lot of crunchy, smelly pleasure for our dogs. They proved to be great snacks and it meant that I didn't have to summon up quite so much inner resolve every time to resist an intense Susie-Belle stare whenever she fancied a little something to eat. Of course she never made any distinction between needing to eat and just wanting to, so there were quite a few stares in a day from her big brown eyes. She had perfected her manipulation of me when it came to her feeding and knew if she gazed at me with a certain look I would nearly always indulge her. I was a complete pushover when it came to this. Michel and I were thankful we had decided at the outset that only one of us would feed her for if she worked her magic on both of us, we would have had double the problem controlling her intake.

As we moved out of winter we made our first trip of the year to France in the spring of the following year. Just as at Christmas, Susie-Belle travelled well in the car and when she entered the house, it was as if she had never been away. We were so surprised to see her go straight to her bed, sit down and look utterly at home; she was happy and it showed. Dogs do this – they show us so completely whether they are happy or sad, they don't fake what they feel. In Susie-Belle's case, once she had started to show us her emotions and we had begun to read them, it was smack-bang obvious to us both how she was feeling at any moment in time. On her arrival in France, it couldn't be mistaken for anything other than what it was and that afternoon as she sat there, full centre on her bed, she was radiating pure contentment.

At home, as well as enjoying longer walks, we had continued to expose her to a variety of different environments. Although our own preference is always open countryside or beach walking with the dogs, we needed to help Susie-Belle to overcome her continuing anxiety about having people around her when she was walking so we interspersed the 'freedom walks' as we dubbed them, where she was off-lead in open space, with others through the town where we live, or the occasional trip to a village or park where on-lead pavement walks were practised. Whilst in France we planned to maintain this with a variety of activity to keep up our efforts at desensitising her to the stresses of traffic noise and people.

We find the spring to be the perfect time to explore the beautiful towns and villages around us that can get overrun with visitors during the summer months. One of my favourite places within easy reach is the medieval fortified town of Saint-Émilion. World famous for its wines, Saint-Émilion is a completely different place in the summer and winter months. In summer the tight cobbled streets are packed with tourists. One July day we visited with Jasmine and disliked the crowded, hectic atmosphere but noted its potential and promised ourselves a return visit. Later that same year at the end of October we took her back there and the place was magical. We were pleased we had sensed its beauty amidst the summer onslaught and not given up on it. It is a UNESCO World Heritage site and out of season in particular, it's easy to see why. Vines have been grown round the town for almost 2,000 years and history oozes from every inch of the place. The architecture is beautifully preserved and views across the landscape are panoramic.

It is not a large town, some refer to it as a village and that spring morning Renae and Susie-Belle had an easy, peaceful walk round the narrow streets enjoying the unique aromas they held. There were a few early visitors wandering about but not enough to make the place feel busy, or ruin its quiet, uncluttered atmosphere. The uneven cobbled streets proved curiously awkward for Susie-Belle until she got used to them as she tottered along. There was a lot of stopping and sniffing at every corner and stone doorway as two little black noses engaged. A full catalogue of canine pee messages were read, interpreted and replied to by the visiting schnauzers. Whilst nose level interested the girls, we enjoyed the breathtaking views over some of the Bordeaux region's most expansive vineyards, which lie right up to the edges of the town. We absorbed the unusual tranquillity of what is a renowned tourist hotspot and felt fortunate that we could bring our dogs to share it with us, even though the focus of their interest was not ours and vice versa.

I don't believe that taking my dogs to a place that is special for us is wasted on them. Although some may think one pavement is as good as another to a dog, for Susie-Belle that morning in Saint-Émilion was special. She was so far away from her previous life, both geographically and metaphorically, in a place redolent with ancient history and still thriving today that I like to think she could sense the continuity of life there. In our continuing efforts to provide her with new stimulation, that morning walk certainly seemed to pique her interest. Whilst we soaked up the atmosphere, enjoyed the architecture, views and history, many centuries worth of aromas that infused the cobbles provided Susie-Belle and Renae with their amusement. We could only imagine what they were sensing but whatever it was, clearly both were happy, satisfied and tired by the time we reached home later that afternoon.

The next day we opted for a local walk closer to home and spent a couple of hours of total delight in warm spring sunshine whilst listening to the sounds of woodpeckers, cuckoos, distant roosters and even a braying donkey. One of our great pleasures in France is being away from constant artificial noise, whether it be traffic, aeroplanes, car alarms, or any of the other annoying blare of crowded suburbia. That morning was perfect – we heard nothing but the simple sounds of nature the entire walk. Susie-Belle was still edgy at home with sudden or loud traffic noise and to see her moving along the footpaths so carefree and happy gave us deep satisfaction. Whilst we knew that we couldn't avoid putting her in places where traffic existed as we have to live where we do in England, we were thankful that we had our regular rural French escapes to provide a welcome antidote. To see the togetherness of Susie-Belle and Renae that morning trotting backwards and forwards with each other along the quiet lanes in happy companionship was simply magical.

Towards the end of our stay we took ourselves out on what we call the long version of the 'Château Walk'. The local big house – I don't know how big a house has to be in France to be classified as a château – is an impressive place, visible from just about everywhere we walk from our modest home. For years it has been the country retreat of a wealthy Bordeaux family. A few years ago when we were back in England one night there was a fire at the château and when we next arrived in France we were shocked to see the blackened remains. It had been such an iconic part of our local landscape, to see it brought down in such devastating fashion was surprisingly distressing for us. Though the damage had been severe the place was in due course restored by local artisans and now once again stands proud and dominant, noble as the local landmark.

We have two versions of our Château Walk: the short and the long. The short walk we do frequently and it takes us past a small lake, across fields lying at the foot of the Château and through chestnut woods back to our place. It's a pleasant, circular four-kilometre walk. In summer the fields are planted with corn and sunflowers, which from a distance look stunning. By the height of summer, as we reach closer and begin our walk through, the beauty is less obvious as the tall plantings create tunnel-like fields and close up are far from appealing.

One hot summer's day with Jasmine, we made the error of crossing a footpath through the cornfield, only to lose her as she shot off the path deep into the corn, probably after a rabbit. We could hear her crashing through the vegetation, getting farther away and for a few minutes my mind raced forwards to a grisly end involving my missing dog. We have seen wild boar come out of the cornfields and I had gruesome visions of Jasmine being dealt with by an angry boar. But I needn't have panicked – Jasmine was never a dog to want to be far from us and soon enough she came running back the way she had gone, looking at us as if to wonder what all the panic was about. Head cocked to one side, her puzzled look said it all: just because *we* didn't know where she was, didn't mean *she* didn't know exactly where we were and it was only a rabbit she was after, not a boar. However, since then it's put me off walking the dogs off-lead through the corn. If it's a hot morning, the short route is the limit of what's possible for an enjoyable walk as the sun beats down on us when we are away from the cool shade of the woods and the walk can quickly get uncomfortably hot.

We took Susie-Belle for her first experience of the long walk since the morning was fresh and cool. This walk is around eight or nine kilometres and takes us round the full perimeter of the Château grounds. Once we reach the other side, we are on the far side of a hill, from where we follow a couple of steep tracks upwards before heading back down through the woods to our tiny house (which never felt tiny until I had walked around a truly large abode). That morning, as we approached the Château, from a distance we could see clouds of dust blowing around the entrance and what sounded like a powerful leaf-blowing machine, an odd sound for that time of year. As we came closer the source of the noise and dust became clear: a man with the biggest leaf-blowing machine I had ever seen was blasting the rough, potholed, chalky lane outside the gates of the Château. This seemed very weird – the fallen leaves would have been a better sight than the newly exposed potholes. But it was clear that special visitors were due that day and the leaves were not welcome. As we passed by, the man studiously continued his task without seeming to notice us. We were relieved that neither Susie-Belle nor Renae seemed perturbed by the noise and curious landscaping.

Whether the activity at the Château distracted us or we were just careless, we took a slightly wrong turn from our usual route and by the time we noticed it was too late, the route we had taken meant that we now had the 'big hill' to climb when our legs were tired at the end of our walk. Usually I make sure we go down the big hill at all times as it's a strain on the legs to do otherwise, but somehow I'd forgotten this essential detail until it was too late. Now we had no choice if we were to make it home, unless we wanted to walk the even longer way round the bottom of it, adding another few kilometres onto an already decent-length walk. At least it wasn't hot – when the sun is out, I break out in a panicky sweat just thinking about that hill if we are on our way home and do all I can to avoid it. So up the hill we went, Susie-Belle and I slowly bringing up the rear, keeping each other company at our own sedate pace. Renae and Michel marched off ahead, for some peculiar reason embracing the steep hill challenge with an energy and enthusiasm I couldn't muster myself and knew Susie-Belle didn't feel. At the top they waited, sat in the cool shade of a cherry tree as we steadily puffed our way up to them.

During that trip Susie-Belle passed a milestone, something we had been waiting for her to achieve for several months: she conquered the staircase. Since she had been with us she had always shown a real reluctance to go up the stairs at home. This it appears is not unusual in puppy farm survivors, they would never have had the early experience of stairs that puppies have and even puppies are wary and can take time to master them. Renae was six months old before she could go up and down with ease. Our house in England is a classic Victorian cottage with a steep staircase with narrow treads (even some human visitors find it initially daunting) so it was no surprise that Susie-Belle was less than keen to tackle it. What was curious with her was that eventually, after several months of coaxing, she would go up them herself, but only ever at night-time when we were headed off to bed. Never in the daytime, even with the same tempting bedtime biscuit being offered.

She had attempted to descend the stairs once, not very successfully and, by the noise she made, had slipped or thrown herself down the last few. After that, I was concerned she might injure herself and felt happier carrying her up to bed and down again in the morning. She never objected to having a little carry round and it was a good opportunity for us to share a cuddle so we were both happy but I still wanted her to feel confident enough to do them alone if she could and continued to encourage her but with no success.

At Christmas she had not mastered the stairs in the house in France but by the spring I knew that she would also have those outside to cope with. We have stairs everywhere – the house is on a hill and the garden is sloped so there are sets of stone steps down to terraces and up to patios, tiled steps up out through the back of the house into the rear courtyard, stairs in the barn to get through to the back gate, as well as indoors the rickety wooden staircase to go up to the bedrooms. If ever Susie-Belle would master moving comfortably up and down stairs, it would be in France. Interestingly, she didn't hesitate the first time she went into the garden that spring. During the Christmas trip she had not really had much of a chance to spend time outside and we hadn't noticed what she had done, but in the warm spring days she was in and out of the house all day, up and down the stairs outside and in the barn without hesitation. I was hopeful that her improving strength and fitness would mean she would tackle those at home if she gained enough confidence in France.

However, her newly discovered agility did not extend to going up and down the indoor staircase. She went up them fine, even during the day if I was upstairs – something she so far never did in the UK. However, she still refused to go down them and I continued to help her and make her life as easy as it could be, carrying her down each morning, or whenever she called at me to give her a hand if she was stuck at the top. I tried leaving her, or encouraging her down with treats, but she could not overcome what seemed to be a complete fear of going down the stairs. To encourage her I waited as long as I dared with her little face pitifully looking down at me and her plaintive bark if I walked off and left her. I did try ignoring her to see if she would conquer her apparent fears but nothing would make her come down, so I always gave in and carried her down. By this time, she had let go of all her earlier tensions about being handled or picked up and was delightfully cuddlesome, relishing any opportunity to be caressed. I was hopelessly being moulded to Susie-Belle's ways and did in the end suspect that she just enjoyed the carry and always obliged, whilst not being fully sure whether she was also really inhibited, if only a touch, by a fear of the stairs. If she enjoyed her sweet manipulation of me, I was happily complicit in her game.

Then I had to return to the UK for a few days, leaving Michel in charge. He said that she did the same with him – she would go up the stairs fine, but not down them, crying and whining to be helped if he left her upstairs. Then, the day that I was due back in the evening, he held out a little longer and just as he was about to give in and go up and once again cuddle her up in his arms, he heard soft, tentative pattering footsteps on the stairs as Susie-Belle made her way carefully down them. She could do it after all and continued to do so from that day onwards... in France. As soon as we arrived back in England, she refused once again to do it herself and fretting that she would hurt herself if she did so reluctantly and enjoying the cuddle we shared in our mutual game, I resumed our ritual of me carrying her down.

CHAPTER EIGHTEEN

A Stormy Night Under Canvas

'This is what we call love. When you are loved, you can do anything in creation. When you are loved, there's no need at all to understand what's happening, because everything happens within you'

– THE ALCHEMIST, *PAUL COELHO*

By the time we returned from France after our spring break, Susie-Belle was showing plenty of signs that she was happier, a lot less timid and fitter. I was certain that she was slowly beginning to trust us and to know that we loved her. She had a serenity that when I sensed it properly for the first time, it seemed to wipe away any fleeting thoughts my mind conjured about whether she was happy or not. Whether she had yet forgotten the torment of her past I couldn't know, but her enjoyment of her new life shone bright and clear. She had been out of the puppy farm for well over a year and with us for eight months and we hoped that she now felt secure enough to know we would never leave her. Her obvious pleasure on returning to France and settling so completely whilst there was reassuring; it seemed she now knew that so long as she was with us, it didn't matter where we all were, she was safe. She wasn't at all fazed by being in different places; my faith in her capacity to rise to the challenge of having a varied way of life seemed to be paying off.

Shortly after our return, we had her next adventure to look forward to, which was also a new one for us: we had decided we would try camping. This would be my first ever experience of life under canvas for I had never done it as a child and once into adulthood had no inclination to see what I had been missing out on. Michel, on the other hand, had been badgering me to camp ever since I had known him. He had happy sun-drenched memories of childhood camps on the beach, carefree and warm. My perception of camping in the UK could not be more different – I had images of being in a state of perpetual cold, wet discomfort and misery, a state I could happily live out my life never experiencing. But I had been chatting to several enthusiastic people who camped around the country and they spoke so highly of the fun they had with their dogs that it tweaked my interest, seeing as I was ever on the lookout for new experiences to share with Susie-Belle.

As we spend July and August in France, camping in the UK for us would never be in the nicer, warmer summer months – if indeed British summers could ever be called warm. Once we had decided to give it a go, we got equipped for cooler camping, thinking that if we prepared for bad weather, we might be pleasantly surprised should our camping days turn out to be hot and dry. However, it just so happened that 2011, the year we decided to camp, coincided with the wettest summer on record. At least we got to try out the mountain of wet weather gear we bought that first year.

Our initial camping weekend also involved another first. We had agreed to take part in the country's inaugural Annual Schnauzer Weekend in the Peak District. The event came about through members of the online UK Schnauzer Forum pooling ideas for a weekend of walks and opportunities to meet up with fellow schnauzer owners. Initially the suggestion came for running a schnauzer camp along the lines of those that happen in some European countries. As the ideas flowed and the weekend took shape people talked about camping and caravanning, staying in hotels and B&Bs, renting cottages and for those close enough to the walks, just making a day trip. As everyone had told us camping with dogs would be fun, with the opportunity to combine it with walking and the companionship of other dogs, it was a weekend we couldn't miss. Susie-Belle was always happiest in the company of dogs – I just hoped she'd like being in a tent too.

The walks for the weekend were centred on Dovedale, a popular dale in the Peak District National Park, set in a stunning location. We had never visited that part of the country before but were glad we had decided to go that weekend. The scenery is fabulous and so different from what we are familiar with in the south of England or in France. As we drove into the region through mile after mile of rolling farmland, woodland and dramatic dales, a sense of entering a very special place settled on us. The scenery was dramatic and it was easy to see why the area has long been attractive to walkers. Despite the poor weather forecast for the weekend, we looked ahead to the next day of walking with high excitement. Before that though we had our first night under canvas to get through, with rain beginning to fall just as we pulled into the campsite.

Our friends Dean and Jolyon had arrived earlier in the day with their dogs, Rupert and Watson. They gave us a hand pitching our tent in the drizzle, with Renae and Susie-Belle keeping watch from the dry comfort of the car. As the evening gloom set in and the rain fell harder, I got colder and wetter and thought about joining the dogs in the car and heading off for a B&B. But once we had set up, the rain eased and we took the dogs for a walk round the site. Watson was by then only sixteen weeks old and cute and playful as a puppy can be. I was curious to see over the weekend how Susie-Belle would engage with him. She and Renae had spent a lot of time with Rupert and we hoped that their easy companionship would help smooth any anxiety she may have with camping and our crowded agenda. That evening, she certainly seemed to take well to having an energetic puppy around and in her own funny little way enjoyed the playful rough and tumbling of the two boys and Renae.

Where Renae and Rupert could play with some vigour and energy, their strength and boisterousness seemed to overwhelm Susie-Belle at times. Although never one to get fully immersed in play, she was definitely showing more signs of joining in when Renae was in full-on play mode. At this stage her engagement involved a lot of rowdy barking from the sidelines with the occasional bumping of bottoms. Watson's clumsy puppy-like attempts at playing with her seemed to suit her best and she responded to his play bows with stiff, awkward little bounces in return. Sharing the dogs' simple enjoyment of being together at the campsite, it was almost possible to ignore the cold and gloom of the evening. I was starting to see why the happy campers who had recommended I try it with the dogs were so keen to persuade me to join their ranks.

After a trip to the pub, at lights out everyone was so tired and content that once tucked in for the night, the bad weather seemed almost insignificant. Having never camped before, as I lay all night listening to the tent being battered by wind and rain, I had no measure by which to gauge how typical this was for a night under canvas. I was pretty sure though that this was a bad night. As the tent poles creaked and strained and the canvas flapped, I wondered if I should worry about the tent collapsing. It wasn't until around 4am that the wind dropped and I managed to doze off that, when I awoke a couple of hours later, I realised that camping can be peaceful if no gale is blowing.

As I dragged myself out of my sleepiness, I was amazed that neither Renae nor Susie-Belle had been in the least perturbed by the meteorological drama of our first night in a tent. As I had lain awake hour after hour listening to the storm, I shone the torch to check how they were doing. I had half-expected to see both shivering with fright, but surprisingly they had snored their way through the noisiest night I had ever experienced. As the morning light broke through, the campsite slowly came to life and it was clear that I had not imagined the extent of the battering our tent had endured. Debris littered the site; piles of broken tent poles and torn canvas were dumped in bins, where tents had been ripped apart during the night. I saw the worst of camping in early season in Britain and I was thankful we had bought well and prepared for the worst. The thought of losing our tent in the middle of the night and the upheaval it would have brought, not to mention the fright for Susie-Belle and Renae it would have caused made me mightily glad our tent had stood up to the storm.

Later in the morning, the light rain that had been falling on and off stopped and we headed out to join those taking part in the first of the weekend walks. We were starting at Dovedale and the route was to follow a riverside path along the River Dove towards the tiny, picturesque village of Milldale. It looked to be a fabulous six- or seven-mile walk through a scenic valley with the crowd of dogs that promised to turn out for the weekend. Estimated numbers expected were around fifty or sixty dogs, mainly schnauzers. Although these days Susie-Belle was a lot more relaxed walking with people, there were a few niggling worries at the back of my mind as to how well she would cope for two days with lots of new people, in new places. Without being able to go back at the end of each day to the sanctuary of our own home was an added challenge. However, I took comfort from the fact that as well as being with Renae, having her friends Rupert and Watson around on the walks and at the campsite would help her to enjoy the adventure.

As we arrived at the meeting point in Dovedale, the dogs were already starting to gather in impressive numbers. Car after car appeared, from which descended a schnauzer – or two or three in some cases. There were lots of miniatures, the occasional standard and a handful of majestic giant schnauzers by the time we set off from the car park. The sight and sound was incredible and the vivacity present that afternoon on the walk was memorable. Amongst many amazing things about the weekend was the ease with which the large number of dogs got along. Humans and dogs alike seemed to thrive in the spirit of the weekend, coming together to enjoy the company of each other in stunning surroundings. As we moved towards Milldale through the spectacular limestone valley, the dogs bounced round whilst their human companions chatted, caught up with old friends and made many new ones. People were staying in various locations around the Peak District and it was interesting to hear how dog-friendly the different accommodations were proving to be. There were only a few hardy campers and from those tucked away in cosy cottages and B&Bs we obtained much sympathy and some amusement for surviving the storm of the previous night.

After descending on the tiny tea-shop at Milldale for welcome refreshments, we slowly made our way back to Dovedale, savouring the surroundings and company. About halfway along the walk we all stopped for a break and snacks, sitting on rocks and taking it easy. The dogs happily milled about and Susie-Belle spent a happy half-hour moving from person to person, gobbling up whatever treats she could scrounge. There was no nervousness around strangers that afternoon, no hesitation to approach, or be approached if she thought they were strangers bearing tasty gifts. Seeing her trot past people, looking relaxed, I was at times overcome with love for her and pleased to see how far she had come on. She seemed happy – purely, simply happy.

The weather had stayed dry and the cooler, overcast conditions proved perfect for the dogs' comfort. Susie-Belle and Renae were both content: Renae's high energy level was gradually tapering whilst Susie-Belle's pace had slowed to a gentle plod by the time we reached the car. She had shown little sign of being anxious during the long walk or amongst the crowd and I silently applauded my brave companion for getting on and enjoying her weekend.

The next day, we woke to a beautiful, if cool morning. The weather had improved dramatically from the previous stormy evening – there had been no rain or wind overnight and the sun began to push its way through the light cloud. The day ahead looked promising. As we ate our stove-cooked breakfast in the open air I began to get a faint hint of the pleasures of camping for humans. Already I had seen what fun it is for dogs although the joys had so far been minimal as far as I was concerned. But in my quest to provide Susie-Belle and Renae with anything they needed for a happy life, I was prepared to continue our camping hobby and sunny mornings would go a long way towards convincing me it was fun.

Susie-Belle certainly seemed to be enjoying herself – she was always the first to want to get into the tent and last to come out. She tucked herself into her bed and radiated joy as she lay looking out at the world from her comfy vantage point. As well as seeing how content she was in the tent and around the camp, another great thing we witnessed that weekend was her truly mingling for the first time and just being happy to hang out around people. On the group walks over the weekend, she was no longer constantly bothered about being at the back or as worried as she had once been about having people behind her. Although there were still traces from time to time during the walks, it was a lot less present than it had ever been up to that point. Thinking back to the early group walks when she had first arrived with us, she had stood stock-still, anxiously looking over both shoulders as people passed her until she was comfortably at the back of the group but she rarely did this at Dovedale. On the long walk from Dovedale to Milldale, she did favour a couple of gentlemen's feet and walked companionably along with them for good stretches but just as much she came forward to catch up with Renae, Rupert and Watson.

That weekend many people commented on how she was doing – some we had met before, others for the first time – and it was such a pleasure to hear strangers remark on how cheerful she appeared to be. The only time that she seemed a little sad the whole weekend was when we had to pack away the tent. In fact we couldn't get her out of it at one stage as she had settled herself comfortably in the middle of it whilst we put away everything around her! It was the cutest sight. Everyone had been right: dogs love to camp and Susie-Belle was no exception.

CHAPTER NINETEEN

Swimming Buddies

Do not be wedded forever
To fear, yoked eternally
To brutishness.

– 'ON THE PULSE OF THE MORNING',
MAYA ANGELOU

Life with Susie-Belle and Renae was shaping up to be a lot of fun, for them and us. Susie-Belle's physical and emotional wellbeing were showing continuing improvement. She was responding well to the treatment for the KCS and her eyes were not causing any concern at our regular checks with Mr Yellowley. Psychologically, she was doing well: after each new thing we tried together, she seemed to grow a little bolder in her day-to-day life.

We liked to plan small adventures with her to go somewhere different, or try something out for the first time, to tweak her curiosity. As we knew her life experiences had been very limited and also extremely nasty, every little thing we did for the first time with her we could be certain was a new exploit in her life. This made her different from many rehomed dogs, where they have lived in homes, in families and may have done things before. For puppy farm survivors their complete existence prior to rescue is lived within a few square miserable metres: they are dogs for whom treading on grass for the first time is a novel experience. With Susie-Belle we embraced the spirit of adventure in its truest, simplest sense: we joined her in pushing ourselves to leave the familiar and tried new things, new places and together we had fun. We did things that she or we wouldn't normally do – simple things that at times were new to just her, others new for us all. Camping was one adventure, another we introduced her to that first summer was one of my favourites: river swimming.

I started swimming outdoors in rivers, lakes and the sea a couple of years before we lost Jasmine. Although she accompanied me on many swimming escapades, she didn't really enjoy getting wet and never willingly joined me whilst I swam. She could be encouraged to swim with me if I carried her out to the middle of the river and played awhile with her, but her enthusiasm was always restrained. On hot summer days in France she would dip her paws for a paddle in the river at the bottom of our hill, but only enough to cool herself down before retreating to the dry safety of the riverbank. During her last summer, when she was too frail and stiff to walk to the bottom of the hill, every afternoon we took her in the car to the river so she could enjoy a spot of river hydrotherapy to soothe her old and aching body. At this stage she seemed to sense that it helped her and as we held her in our arms against the gentle current, we would feel her relax as she rhythmically stretched and curled, and uncurled her limbs in the cool waters.

Renae was showing no sign of being a keen swimmer. In fact she was completely averse to being anywhere near water, stepping round puddles, skipping out of the way of stray hose sprinkles and enduring the occasional bath. Her first summer with us, whilst Susie-Belle was recuperating from cataract surgery with Janet, I did a lot of swims in the UK as well as France and hoped that if we encouraged Renae from puppyhood, she would be eager to join me. It hadn't worked. Maybe my obsessive intensity had overwhelmed her. I'd spent a lot of time pestering her to sample the sea and rockpools in Cornwall one sunny June weekend. The numerous onlookers with dogs rushing happily in and out of the waves watched in bewilderment my coercive efforts at getting my puppy to join me. My humiliation was complete when she ran off up the beach to the lifeguards as soon as she could.

Michel kept urging me to take it slowly and let her join in my aquatic adventures if and when she wanted to, but I wanted her to do it now and kept pushing her to join in the fun. Only she wasn't seeing it as fun – she clearly couldn't understand what I was doing whenever I stripped off and strode into the fresh waters of the local river at home. She would run along the river path barking at me whilst I swam in the green cool waters of the River Wey, keeping as far from the edge of the bank as she could. Even when we met Labradors, retrievers and spaniels all jumping in and out of water, whether at the beach or river, chasing sticks or diving for balls, she wouldn't join in. As soon as her paws hit moisture, she would withdraw, stop the game and wait for them to join her back on dry land. If ever there was a puppy not keen on swimming, Renae was it. Mismatched with a human companion who loved nothing better than jumping into any body of outside water she could find.

Having seen Susie-Belle in the middle of winter in France wade confidently into a flooded stream without hesitation, I was hopeful that I might at last have found a canine swimming companion. Although schnauzers are not a breed known for their affinity with water, at the Annual Schnauzer Weekend in the Peak District, a few had revelled in splashing in and out of the River Dove. One little black mini, Arthur, properly swam, repeatedly diving under the water. He had to be strongly encouraged to end his swim and continue the walk. I saw Arthur and desperately wanted Susie-Belle and I to join him and share his abundant joy of swimming. If I had brought my swimsuit and there hadn't been several hundred people milling around that day, I would certainly have been in there with him. Admittedly Susie-Belle had shown no inclination to join in the fun but I was hoping that was down to her natural reserve rather than a water aversion.

A week or so after Dovedale, one evening after work we joined some outdoor swimming friends down near Southampton. They regularly swim in the gorgeous, tidal River Hamble and have a quiet, secluded spot where they swim. As we were intending to cover some distance rather than dip and float by the bank, Susie-Belle couldn't swim with me but I was keen to see if she would paddle as I set off. The evening was warm but the water was cool and, as I headed out into the river with the others, I glanced back over my shoulder to see Susie-Belle waist-deep at the water's edge. Michel had stayed back on the riverbank with her and Renae as he wasn't swimming and he watched her stand there with her gaze fixed out to water the whole time I was away. She went into the water as deep as she could without swimming and as she spotted me returning to the shore an hour or so later started barking excitedly. I don't know what was going through her mind as she stood there seeing me disappear under the water to reappear farther downstream and then disappear again from sight. Whilst Susie-Belle kept a vigilant, I hope not anxious but perhaps puzzled, watch for my return, Renae wandered along the bank ignoring the waterside activity with her back pointedly turned to the water. Any hope I had of having company in my swimming adventures that summer clearly lay with Susie-Belle.

A short while later we were back in France again with a series of river explorations planned before the summer crowds arrived to spoil the tranquillity. Our region has many popular rivers and lakes and in summer the better-known ones can become busy with holidaying visitors and locals. We wanted to explore some of the wilder ones off the beaten track and, armed with our map and swimming gear, ventured south in search of a selection of perfect river swims. One of the most idyllic we found that trip was on the River Vézère, about two hours from our house, made perfect by Susie-Belle joining me for the first of many magical swims that summer.

The River Vézère runs through one of Europe's most important prehistoric sites. The Vézère Valley is where the world famous Lascaux Cave is found, along with over 140 other prehistoric sites. The river meets the more famous Dordogne at the village of Le Bugue and we swam just upstream of that, near the ancient village of Tursac. To get to the river we parked under the dark shade of some oak trees and crossed on foot a heavily overgrown field. It was distinctly less appealing than it had looked on the map, especially with two small dogs in tow and a heap of stuff to carry. By the time we had scrambled with our picnic and swimming gear through waist-high nettles and brambles, clearing the path as we went, I was in desperate need of a refreshing float downstream. At one point I had scooped Susie-Belle up under one arm, slung my swimming bag over my shoulder, with picnic mat in hand to lift her through the worst of the overgrowth. Renae bounced ahead, not bothered by the thicket we were struggling to get through. If she'd known it was all to reach a river for a swim, she may have been less enthusiastic and able-bodied and hung at the back to scupper my plan. Eventually, reaching the end of the path, I put Susie-Belle down and compliant as ever, she followed our footsteps down to the edge of the river, which when we saw where we were made the tussle through the field all worthwhile.

Access to the river was awkward but once there we were richly rewarded. The dark river ran at the base of overhanging limestone cliffs, along which perched high up above the water was an ancient troglodyte village. There's evidence that people have lived in this area since Neanderthal times and that day it was easy to sense the primordial nature of the place. Although the day was hot and the midday sun was high in the sky, the overhanging cliffs and thick canopy of trees from the riverbank blocked much of the light. As we looked upstream, shafts of sunlight shone through the leaves to sparkle on the water's surface, catching the swift fluttering movements of dragonflies going undisturbed about their day. As I looked up at the steep cliffs I imagined the history this stretch of river had witnessed. The settlements were perched high to avoid attacks from the river by Vikings and later the English in The Hundred Years War. It was amazing to sense the spirit of the place and marvel at the endless cycle of life it embodied. Hot and sticky from our scramble through the fields, we settled ourselves at the edge of the river, hearing only birds and the soothing sounds of the water and in cool, dark seclusion, stripped off and plunged into the refreshing waters.

During the height of the summer, the river level drops but that day it was perfect for swimming – deep enough but not too fast-flowing. As we splashed and swam and cooled off, Renae sniffed her way along the water's edge, taking care to avoid getting her paws wet. Susie-Belle, on the other hand, waded in to join us but stopped just as she got waist-deep, as in the River Hamble. We watched and waited for her to swim over as she seemed keen to join us but she couldn't do it – she couldn't bring herself to move out of her depth.

After waiting a while, I decided to help her, judging she looked happy enough in the water and hadn't hesitated to enter it. What was stopping her swimming farther was the fact that she had never had the chance to swim and be out of her depth before. As she had never swum in her life she didn't know that she could do it. So I lifted her up and carried her with me into the deeper waters at the centre of the river. I was careful to sense if she stiffened or became stressed in any way but she seemed happy to be with me as I held her secure in my arms. Together we floated in the softly moving, magical waters under the overhanging cliffs. Susie-Belle and I were adding our piece of history to the river that day. Never before had this little dog swum but swim she did right then with me. As I gently released her from my arms, her paws started paddling, smoothly, confidently and beautifully. She swam away from me towards Michel; she was a natural in the water and it was a moment we will forever cherish. On land she was still a bit stiff and awkward in her movements but in the water she was fluid, graceful and wonderful to watch. Seeing her move happily across the river, she resembled an otter, her beautiful head held perfectly above the surface of the water, her paws paddling rhythmically. How far away she was that day from the horrors of her past, how far she had travelled with us to enjoy her first swim, how brave she was to have journeyed to this point. I was certain that she celebrated her well-earned freedom in her first proper river swim that day.

I have often been told that dogs are natural swimmers and that they can all do it. However, I know this is not true. Where Susie-Belle clearly is a natural, we also have Renae: she cannot swim and is very unwilling to learn. We have patiently tried to teach her, to help her to see that she need not panic and try to run across the surface of the water, but she has no wish to share aquatic pleasures and insists on frantically splashing her way out of any water she finds herself in. I now accept that she is best left to her own devices on the riverbank and I watch her peacefully entertain herself with the sights and smells of the bank. But I do have my swimming companion for that summer Susie-Belle spent many happy days with me in the rivers and every time she swam she was like an elegant plump grey otter.

I know it may seem to some that just because I love to swim and be in water, I shouldn't force this on my dogs but I know that if I hadn't offered Susie-Belle the opportunity to swim her way through that first summer with us, she would never have known what joy she was missing. She was never forced into water – she always followed me in freely. By offering our dogs the chance to experience it, they can now both choose what they do when we are at the riverbank. We accept that Renae is not going to swim – she is happy just to potter along the bank, enjoying her time her own way. But Susie-Belle, now she knows what swimming is and knows she can do it, willingly joins us, not every time, but when she wants to she does. When she swims I feel something wonderful happening as I believe that every time she does so, she grows a little happier. If that's me projecting my own feelings, I can live with that.

CHAPTER TWENTY

Growing Expectations

'If you find it in your heart to care for somebody else, you will have succeeded'
– 'WHERE WE BELONG, A DUET', *MAYA ANGELOU*

Every day with Susie-Belle we were seeing subtle changes in her which showed us that she was really becoming the dog she could always have been, had fate treated her more kindly. Where initially she had been reserved and timid now she was increasingly starting to engage not only with us but with others too. Renae had always gone for one morning a week to a local day-care place for dogs, where she got to socialise, play all morning in the fields, have fun with the agility equipment and have an all-round great time. Before Susie-Belle joined us, I had discussed with Janet whether she thought it would be a good idea or too overwhelming for Susie-Belle to attend with Renae, who loved it. I gave it a lot of thought and did have concerns that it might be too scary for her to really benefit from it, and I did worry that her special needs may not be properly understood. After speaking with Bruce, the owner, and Mark, the wonderful chap who collects Renae and takes care of her whilst she's at the centre, I decided on balance Susie-Belle would benefit from it, for the same reasons that Renae does. Before I let Mark take her, however, I sat him down and gave him a full set of precise instructions as to how Susie-Belle needed to be looked after. No one was to rush her, touch her in a hurried or abrupt fashion, coerce her into anything, stand behind her if she didn't want them to, or firmly handle her. Never, ever were they to even mildly raise a voice to her, even if trying to get her to move or do something. When Susie-Belle doesn't want to move, she won't – she will sit her bottom down and won't budge until she is ready. The worst thing anyone could do to her at that stage would be to use force or drag her. She needs to move in her own time when she has worked out that there really is nothing to worry about. This I needed Mark to understand and straightaway he got it. Above all else Susie-Belle was absolutely always to be treated as a special guest. Nearly all of this was unnecessary for me to say as I had complete confidence and trust in everyone who had looked after Renae there, but it felt important to make sure that Susie-Belle's special needs were known. Only when I was certain that everyone understood that she was not a normal dog, or even a typical rescue dog, but one that required particular consideration did I agree to her accompanying Renae on her once-a-week morning out. I saw attending day-care as a useful part of her programme of recovery but needed to be secure that everyone else involved saw it that way too.

Every Tuesday when Mark appeared to collect the two dogs

I would secretly watch him patiently walk Susie-Belle down the garden path, stopping every now and then to give her a little stroke under her chin if she was in one of her slower moods. With us she has always had her own pace of life and we respect that and to see Mark intuitively do this too was touching. I could see that he understood her as he let her take her time. Sometimes I would go out with them to see her off, but more and more I was happy to let Mark take her alone with Renae. Watching her with Mark, I was heartened to know that she was perfectly content to go out for the morning independently with him and her sister. She was not going to day-care just to fill the time, she was going as part of our programme of helping her to live as fulfilled and happy a life as she deserved. Renae had thrived through her experiences there and I hoped Susie-Belle would enjoy it just as much. An overdependence on primary carers easily develops in ex-puppy farm dogs and part of my reasoning for choosing to send Susie-Belle to day-care was to allow her the experience of being with others who took good care of her, away from me.

Every time Mark came back with them, I grilled him on how Susie-Belle had got along, what she had behaved like and if there had been any problems. I got feedback from him and regular updates from others on how she was settling in and all was pleasing to hear. Mark spoke of how some days Renae would be off running and playing with her day-care pals, whilst Susie-Belle was content to take it in her own time, mooching round the fields, enjoying the company of humans and dogs alike. But Renae never forgot her sister was there and would frequently break off her games to check on Susie-Belle or to join her for a quieter morning's activity. The sisters would frequently be in the company of one another and when every session ended, Mark said that wherever Renae was, she would always join Susie-Belle before making the short trip home to me.

Although day-care would not be appropriate for every dog with Susie-Belle's background, and not all day-care would have been right for her, with Renae as company it was the right decision to send her, of this I have no doubts. It helped her to gain a small sense of independence in the secure company of Renae, who has been going to the centre ever since she was a young puppy. I made sure that those looking after her knew what she needed and only when I was satisfied this was understood and would be provided would I let her go. Although in Susie-Belle we have never really seen a distinct preference for female company, this is a common trait in puppy farm survivors, who are often more anxious around men than women. Mark has been amazing with her and to have another male in her life she can trust and be happy in the company of is always going to be positive.

As the months with Susie-Belle passed, we saw steady progress and every week noticed and commented on what a happy dog she was becoming. Dogs thrive on routine and consistency as it gives them a sense of stability and expectation in their world. So whilst we share a varied life with Susie-Belle, within that we maintain a core set of daily routines and times. Our early morning pattern is always the same, irrespective of any other plans we have for the day we go out for a decent walk before doing anything else. In the early days Susie-Belle soon knew what to expect when we came down in the morning: we were heading out. Whether it's a day at home, in France, at friends or camping, we keep with this routine. Likewise meals are given at set times whatever else is going on. By keeping basic things stable on a daily basis even with the variety we added, we believe it minimised any confusion

Susie-Belle may have felt about her new life and helped her to settle well in the first few months.

Another benefit of keeping to a clear routine was that it not only helped her to feel secure, it also encouraged a sense of expectation to grow within Susie-Belle. This is such a normal thing for most dogs to display and an obvious sign of a happy dog, but it was completely absent in Susie-Belle when she first arrived with us. She just didn't show any signs that she could expect to do anything other than spend the day at home on her bed. After all, how could she possibly know that she had a whole rich life now to get on and enjoy? Although constantly observing what was going on around her, she didn't pick up on any signs that exciting happenings like a walk were about to occur. Even though she had spent six months at Janet's, a good amount of that time had been spent resting, gaining health and recuperating from her surgery. Then just as she was getting stronger and more settled in Janet's routines and may have started to anticipate things, we whisked her away from her fledgling sense of security to begin a new set of routines all over again. Whilst we've never been keen on getting Renae excited when preparing to leave the house, there are always regular signs that a walk is about to happen, but it was striking how Susie-Belle would not react to any indicators of us going out that Renae would always be on the lookout for. It was quite a while before picking up their leads would trigger any recognition in Susie-Belle that this meant we were ready for a walk. With her we found we had to actively encourage her that when the signs of going out for a walk were there, she could expect to be invited to enjoy the outside world with us.

We were seeing a lot fewer signs of any anxiety related behaviour and it was the little things that we began to observe that truly showed us Susie-Belle was becoming a normal dog capable of expressing herself and her needs. One day on our afternoon walk she did something that is so common in schnauzers but which we had never seen her do before. It wasn't until she did it that we realised it had been missing up until then. I'm sure it is not a schnauzer-specific thing, but one thing that Jasmine hated (and Renae too) is to have any leaf, twig, or greenery attach itself to their legs, feet or tummy. Both Jasmine and Renae would be instantly immobilised should this happen and stand staring expectantly up at us until we stooped down to remove the annoying attachment before merrily trotting on. Many times Jasmine would have to be frisked to find and remove the tiniest leaf that was annoying her before she would move on. Susie-Belle had never done this: she would just stop and pull off anything clinging to her undercarriage and carry on walking once she'd dealt with it. She never expected to have help with such trifles. Unsurprising when in the puppy farm there would never have been help available for what would have been bigger problems than an annoying attached leaf. After all, this was a dog who had undoubtedly given birth without assistance to multiple litters – a twig caught in her hair was not going to be much of a bother for Susie-Belle to deal with alone. That was until that afternoon when she stood stock-still, wouldn't budge and looked at me with the exact same expression on her face that I had seen over the years from Jasmine. I was so moved as it was such a fine demonstration of her willingness now to ask for my help; to recognise she didn't have to put up with something or manage on her own.

The little pause on our walk because a leaf was irritating her showed me that now she not only trusted me to help her, but also expected me to do so. For the first time in her life Susie-Belle had gained a sense of expectation and my heart sang out in celebration. This was a major breakthrough in her rehabilitation, in her journey towards being a normal dog. After I had bent down and picked off the offending greenery, I hugged her with an enthusiasm that must have been utterly baffling to her.

CHAPTER TWENTY-ONE

Dragged Backwards
by a Clip

'Find ecstasy in life; the mere sense of living is joy enough'
– EMILY DICKINSON

As our life with Susie-Belle continued, we learned more and more what we enjoyed doing together and what was best for helping Susie-Belle to enjoy her life to the widest possible point. We liked to plan small adventures with her to go somewhere different just to pique her interest and avoid at all costs tedium touching her life ever again. I'd never have imagined how much she would enjoy camping and being in a tent with us but she wholeheartedly did. She was such a sweetheart whenever we camped, always being first to inspect the tent interior and last to leave at the end.

Though struggling to reach the level of enthusiasm for camping that Renae and Susie-Belle clearly showed, I relished the thought of finding something that Susie-Belle so clearly enjoyed and was happy to set aside my reservations and throw myself into our new hobby. We planned to make a series of short camping trips until it got too cold in the autumn to be worth doing. Seeing as how we had started our camping season in just about the stormiest conditions possible and still not hated it, we were game for as much as we could fit in; all in the cause of creating as much enjoyment for Susie-Belle in her lifetime as we could.

After the Dovedale trip, next up was a camp on the South Coast at Hastings. The weekend was arranged a few weeks in advance and the girls would once again have the company of Rupert and Watson in the tent next door. As the weekend approached, we looked with disbelief at the weather forecast: gale force winds were expected to batter the South Coast on Friday night. We couldn't believe our misfortune – two camps and two stormy weekends, this was really testing our resolve and commitment to camping with Susie-Belle. If we hadn't already made arrangements with Dean and Jolyon, I doubt we would have ventured to the coast. As it was, we were very tempted to cancel the trip and stay at home but a quick cajoling message from Dean on the morning we were due to go persuaded us to stick with the plan and off we headed, hoping the forecasters had got it wrong. About half an hour from home on the motorway we drove through a torrential downpour best described as an English version of a monsoon. A sense of maniacal humour overtook us as we envisioned pitching our tent in weather most people wouldn't venture out in, let alone hunker down for a camp. As we shouted at each other to be heard over the crazy racket of the rain on the roof of the car, Susie-Belle and Renae sat up, puzzlement writ all over their faces. It seemed we weren't the only ones in the car wondering if a touch of madness was in the air that day.

As we neared Hastings, the rain suddenly stopped as quickly as it had started and we drove into the campsite under a remarkable clear blue sky. It was hardly believable that only an hour before, the sky had dumped gallons of summer rain on us. As we moved through the campsite to find Dean and Jolyon, it seemed the ominous forecast had kept wiser campers at home as it was completely deserted save for one tent in a far field and one caravan. We had the pick of the site and were glad we had come as the space and freedom would be perfect for the dogs to enjoy once we'd set up. Although there was no sign of rain, the wind was picking up and we hurried to get our tents up whilst the dogs played freely and ran round the enormous deserted site.

Seeing Susie-Belle join in the fun, playing with young Watson whilst Renae and Rupert rough and tumbled together and chased at high speed, I pushed away any doubts about whether camping that weekend had been the right decision. Susie-Belle was learning to show her enjoyment and almost play; she would still stand on the sidelines and bark and bark at times, but increasingly she was starting to show signs that she knew that this was play and that she could even join in. Watching her at the campsite that afternoon, she was animated and fully engaged in the fun created by having the additional company of Rupert and Watson. Even if gale force winds rocked the site that night, the rollicking time the dogs were having would be more than worth it. As it turned out, the winds did howl all night and I lay awake for most of it, fretting over the morning scenes from the Peak District of torn tents and broken poles, but mercifully our tent held out once more and we woke unscathed to a calm, sunny morning. Yet again I was amazed at how at ease and peaceful the dogs had been all night in the noisy tent. They were definitely natural, happy campers and for once they were both streets ahead of me in learning new tricks, like sleeping through storms when there's just a thin sheet of canvas as protection.

We had been invited to walk with Mike and Sharon, who live with their dogs in Hastings. They had planned a couple of scenic routes to show us their favourite places, the first of which was Rye Harbour Nature Reserve. A designated Site of Special Scientific Interest, this large coastal reserve has lots to interest dogs as well as humans, with spreading shingle beaches, grassland, saltmarshes, huge expanses of sand at low tide and a network of paths. Mike is a brilliant amateur photographer and takes hundreds of photographs of his and other dogs exploring the reserve and we were really keen to take the girls out there, despite the blustery day.

For a good couple of hours we battled the cool north-easterly wind and accompanied the dogs on their quest to make the most of the Site of Special Smells of Interest to which we had brought them. When their noses weren't stuck in the sand or shingle, they were hurtling round, playing tag with each other on the vast sandy beach. Susie-Belle didn't join in with the chasing but she was certainly fully wrapped up in the spirit of the weekend, showing little inhibition around the people on the beach and happily going up to Mike, who she hadn't previously met, throughout the walk.

Mike's photographs record a day of superb fun for all the dogs, but those of Susie-Belle are particularly moving to look back at. As she stands strong against the coastal wind, her face lifted to the sky, she looks truly bursting with happiness. For those who doubt whether dogs can smile, they definitely do – Mike's photographs are unambiguous testament to this. The wind kept us company all weekend but it stayed dry and by the end of it we went home happy, having shared with Renae and

Susie-Belle a perfect time of walks, beachside fish and chips, and good company. Camping was fast becoming a highlight of Susie-Belle's life and my previous resistance to its charms was starting to crumble in the face of her pleasure. Whatever she was gaining and learning from her life with us, we were also benefiting from being alongside her on her journey.

One of the regular chores that I had to get Susie-Belle familiar with was being comfortable with being groomed and it took several months and attempts to reach a stage where she was reasonably at ease with this. Schnauzers are a breed with high grooming needs and must be clipped regularly and brushed several times a week to prevent matting. In the battery farms, none of this would get done – dogs with long coats come out with horrendous urine-soaked, matted coats. In those places of torment all dogs suffer but for those with high or moderate grooming requirements, whose coats don't shed but mat, having the knotted, filthy, painful coats to cope with was an added indignity. When rescued, they must undergo the trauma of learning to be groomed for their own wellbeing, not for fashionable ends. Even if kept short, their fur needs to be kept brushed; to keep it short, it must be clipped. For dogs unused to handling and where having a lead put on is a major hurdle, the stress that simple grooming can provoke is sad to witness, even sadder to be responsible for inflicting.

Before she came to us, Janet had ensured that Susie-Belle got used to being bathed and groomed. Her wonderful volunteer Claire, who grooms all her fosterers with the sensitivity and patience they need, had given her a tidy up just before leaving for her new life with us. Although we love schnauzers, we are not in the least bit concerned whether or not our schnauzers have the typically groomed style of the breed and for many years I had managed Jasmine's grooming myself and continued this with Renae. When Susie-Belle came along, there was no way that I could have entrusted this to anyone, knowing how stressed it might make her. I left it a long time before I myself gained sufficient courage to give her the first of what would be a lifetime of home grooming sessions with me. When I first attempted it, she was shaggy but not matted for I had brushed her regularly enough to avoid this. Perhaps the only advantage of her dismally thin coat was that in the months that it took to thicken up and threaten to mat, she had relaxed enough for me to attempt her first clipping.

During the winter months of mud-soaked walks, out of necessity I had given her a few baths during which she had been relatively relaxed. As she didn't seem to mind water, I think this helped her to accept that a warm bath was nothing to be too bothered by. From time to time I had taken the scissors to odd bits of excessive fur to keep a semblance of tidiness and hygiene for her but avoided getting the clippers out. We eventually reached the stage though where I could no longer put off a proper clipping and a more thorough tidy. I chose a day when we had little else planned, when I could take my time, help her to relax and if necessary, do it in several short stints with breaks in between.

At this stage Susie-Belle had grown comfortable with me handling her and at times felt distinctly relaxed if we were cuddling. It was getting to be quite a decent length of time before she would wriggle and wish to move away. The days of her front limbs splaying wide and throwing her head back stiff in terror seemed a distant memory; on occasion she even relaxed within moments of me picking her up. From our early days together I had continued the frequent massage sessions and she now unambiguously enjoyed this, encouraging me with her deep sighs and pressing against my hands. We would lie together, Susie-Belle on her bed in front of the fire, me on the floor beside her, and I'd work rhythmically along her neck, down her back and round her flanks, gently massaging the muscles, teasing out any traces of tension. By the summer, when the fire was no longer in use, she would sit on her bed looking at me, without shifting her gaze and I grew to understand that this look was her way of requesting a cuddle, a massage and some attention. Although it would still be several months before she confidently approached me for some stroking she had settled into the tactile nature of our home with a quiet, profound appreciation that I could not have imagined when she first arrived.

The day of her first proper groom, I set up the room and first gave Renae a tidy up so that Susie-Belle could see there was nothing to worry about. Renae had always loved being clipped. Her enjoyment of brushing was a little more hit and miss: some days she would be an angel, others more devil-like but when it came to the clippers she was never a problem. If I got the timing right, she would even drift off into a light sleep with my hand supporting her head and the other clipping. Any professional groomer watching my amateur techniques would have been less than impressed at the amount of cuddling that went on and the time it took me to complete but it worked for us and that was all that mattered. I hoped Susie-Belle would pick up on her sister's vibe and be equally calm. Popping her onto the table, I gently started, trying to impart a confidence I wasn't sure that I really felt. Firstly I worked over the easiest bits with the scissors to get her used to the process and my close attention. As she seemed to be coping with this, I introduced the clippers, moving slowly and lightly over her body, prioritising the longest, scruffiest areas and removing the odd mat that I found. She didn't want to stand and kept lying down, hanging her head low, which reminded me of how she had looked when she first arrived. I adapted my method to move the clippers over her whilst she lay, just lifting her up when I needed to. But I avoided her belly, which was still almost bare, exposing her grossly enlarged nipples that through years of use had swollen beyond normal. It would be a long while before they started to shrink.

As the minutes passed and her fur came off, I sensed that Susie-Belle was not relaxing as Renae does as the clipping goes on; she was hunching herself into a tighter ball, keeping her head low and her limbs tucked under her. Time to stop. I decided to abandon my original plan to take frequent breaks and start and stop until I had done what I considered a good enough clip. Seeing her on the table, she seemed to be regressing to a state of tension I hadn't seen in a long while with her. So I called it a day and didn't much care if she didn't look very schnauzer-like. To take a break and get her up on the table again that day would not have been the right thing to do. For now, she was tidy enough. I had removed the worst of the shagginess and we would have another attempt a few weeks later when she was ready.

The day had shown me that whilst she was making excellent progress in many ways, Susie-Belle's anxious responses were not far off. Although many days they felt a long way behind us and we barely remembered how she was at the beginning, it was clear that her fears were still lurking, ready to reappear if the trigger was there. The monstrous years of torture weren't going to give up their hold on her just yet.

CHAPTER TWENTY-TWO

Fruit Salad Days

*'Dogs are our link to paradise. They don't know evil or
jealousy or discontent. To sit with a dog on a hillside on a
glorious afternoon is to be back in Eden'*
– MILAN KUNDERA

Susie-Belle's first long summer holiday to France came
almost a year after she had been with us. The summer that
year in the UK was dismal, incessantly cold and the wettest on
record; we were looking forward to being outside under blue
skies and enjoying some longed-for warmth. We had been for
short trips in early summer and knew that Susie-Belle would
be happy spending August mornings at the lake and
afternoons by the river but I was a little concerned as to how
she would cope if we had too many scorching-hot days. On
the odd day we'd had some warmth in England she had
seemed uncomfortable, which quickly escalated into rapid

panting to cool herself. In late July we packed the car, closed the house in England and headed over the Channel to the peace and warmth of Susie-Belle's first French summer.

After leaving Calais, we sped through a landscape that became less green and lush the further south we went as fields of sunflowers began popping up, urging us towards warmer days. As we moved out of the damp clutches of the northern half of France the grass verges had a crisp, dusty brown look about them and, with some hope, we looked ahead to the long sunny days and bright skies that had been so scarce at home. The temperature gauge on the car had been steadily rising throughout the long drive and as we arrived at the house in the late afternoon we got out of the cool, air-conditioned interior to be hit not just by warmth but scorching heat. Renae and Susie-Belle were keen to escape the confines of the car but as soon as they stepped into the burning heat of the overgrown garden, their pink tongues were hanging long and loose as both sought rapid shelter in the shade under the low, drooping branches of the lime tree. I wondered what might be going through their minds as they lay gently panting on the shaded grass, noses raised, sniffing the dry hot air. They had left England in the early hours of a cool, drizzly morning to end their day in the rude shock of the heat of high summer in southwest France.

Before we set about unpacking the car, we settled them in the cool of the shuttered house until the heat subsided as evening fell. Later, after we had sorted things in the house we ventured into the courtyard at the back to enjoy our first properly warm summer evening of the year. Surrounded on three sides by the stone walls of the house and facing south, the courtyard is a sun trap made unbearably hot during the day but perfect in the evenings. All day long the walls and stonework on the ground absorb the relentless heat, to release it steadily into the cooling night air. This takes the chill off the evening as we lie back on our loungers in the dark, star gazing, listening to the sounds of the countryside at night. But until the night is cool and properly dark, the radiant heat from the stone makes it still too warm to sit comfortably there during the hottest times in August until well into the night.

That first evening, the air was sticky and warm and heady with the sweet scent of jasmine wafting from plants which scramble abundantly along walls around the house. We gave Jasmine her name as it is one of our favourite summer flowers and we brought her home to us immediately following a holiday in Turkey, where it grew everywhere, scenting the hot nights. Now when our plants release their exquisite perfume at dusk into the garden air in France, it provokes many happy memories of our time with her. We were very tired after the journey but the perfume was enticing and as darkness fell the sky became an incredible sight. It was all too good to miss by going indoors to bed, so we lay out on the loungers and relished the amazing night sky, free from the light pollution that blights the crowded corner of England that we call home.

Susie-Belle and Renae sat with us, unaware of the shimmering night beauty above, but acutely alert to the sounds of the night all around us. Every now and again, one or both of them would erupt into a noisy frenzy of barking as some sound, distant or close, grabbed their attention. We often wonder whilst we're enjoying the peace and dark of the summer night garden in France, why Renae and Susie-Belle never just lay quietly as they do every evening indoors or even outdoors in England. Often they are super alert, senses primed, ready to burst into noisy activity when whatever it is that remains a mystery to us stirs them into responding. We can only guess that without the disruptive light and background sounds of suburbia they are used to, they are better able to react to the unfamiliar noises of the natural world. Whilst it seems to us that they are reacting to nothing, it is more likely that their better night vision and acute hearing gets a chance to work in ways rarely enjoyed in England. Dogs can hear sounds at much higher frequencies than us, and whilst we cannot hear the nocturnal creatures going about their nightly routines, our dogs most certainly can.

That first night laying out in the garden as we soaked up the stunning night sky and jasmine aroma, thoughts of them being too sleepy to stay out after their long day were quickly dispelled as Susie-Belle and Renae absorbed and responded to the high pitched sounds of the night, undetectable to our human ears. They were excited, alert and vocal. We were pleased there were no neighbours nearby to hear the cacophony of noise drowning out the previous peace in the darkened courtyard. As we eventually headed off to bed, I hoped that familiarity each night over the next few weeks would breed certain contempt for the sounds of the nocturnal countryside and that we wouldn't have a repeat performance of noisy alertness every evening.

The sun that had been so elusive in England was in abundance in our corner of France that summer trip and we didn't get a drop of rain the whole time we were there. Often in July and August there will be the odd day when it clouds over, or the heat builds up until it dramatically breaks in a crashing thunderstorm, but there was none of that and we didn't have a day when the sky wasn't blue. It was really perfect weather for a few weeks and we were very thankful indeed – especially when we heard how persistently cold and wet the British summer remained. With constant sun, the challenge each day was to keep Susie-Belle and Renae both cool and exercised. During Susie-Belle's first visit in the depths of winter each day we had walked for miles through the stark landscape around the house but this wasn't possible in August. At that time of year despite rising early to catch the best of the fresh morning cool before the day heats up we are rarely able to walk far before the sun makes it too uncomfortable. Even waiting till past nine o'clock in the evening it is often still too warm for more than a slow wander along the lane by the house. On the hottest days, after an alfresco lunch, we retreat indoors for the afternoon behind closed shutters that keep the house as cool as the best air-conditioning system ever could.

In Jasmine's last couple of years on hot days she had been happy to potter round the garden and take short walks in the fields around the house, but with Renae's high energy level to exhaust and Susie-Belle's need to keep improving her fitness we knew that we couldn't spend several weeks of lazy days with no activity. By the end of the holiday, Renae would be bored and unfit, Susie-Belle and I would be unfit and fat. So, most mornings we went out to a lake that is a short drive away for a morning swim and walk through the surrounding pine forest. In August the lake can be very busy with visitors and locals and we prefer to avoid it at those times. In the years when we first visited, the lake was free of notices listing endless rules and regulations but over time these have crept in. Officially dogs are not permitted near the lake edge, or to swim, and there is a designated marked-up swimming area for people, where lifeguards keep watch in the height of the season. But until mid-morning when people start arriving it is usually deserted and we can swim alone and in peace, blissfully ignoring the arbitrary rules.

Some days we were early enough to swim before the sun rose, slipping into the silky, warm water and sending gentle ripples across the glassy surface. It always feels such a privilege to break the water's surface when it is so still and perfect. Other mornings a breeze would blow across the water, producing a light chop to our swims. Every morning was different and each one was special. Whilst we dipped, Susie-Belle would stand at the water's edge, content to walk in and out cooling her feet, watching us swim. The lake is sandy bottomed, keeping the water warm and the colour of milky tea. Away from the popular beach area and designated swimming area, it is thickly lined with reeds, becoming swampy at the farthest end away from the visitors. On days when I fancied a long swim, I'd head off across the lake, feeling faintly subversive as I ducked below the marker ropes to resurface farther out towards the middle of the lake and swim up to the murk, leaving Michel with the girls for the hour or so it took me to go end to end. Susie-Belle would give an occasional bark as I went away into the distance before settling herself down to keep watch for my return. When she spotted me swimming back to shore, she'd jump up, paddle into the shallow water at the lake edge and serenade my safe return with excited barking. More often than not, Renae busied herself checking out the smells around the pine trees, steadfastly ignoring the watery temptations of the lake but alerted by Susie-Belle would manage to bring herself closer as I arrived back at shore, though never quite wetting her paws.

Depending on the time, morning temperature and how we felt, either before or after swimming we would walk for an hour or so through the shade of the forest. Renae and Susie-Belle never tired of exploring the area – every day there would be a change of smells. Over the weeks, they got used to the morning routine and led by their noses we happily let them decide which pathway through the forest they wanted to take.

Mostly Susie-Belle would follow the route chosen by her sister, who trotted purposefully from tree to tree, working her way through the forest bordering the lake. On the hottest mornings, inferior as they are, even our noses would twitch and respond to the magic of forest aromas as we picked up the distinct smell of pine resin in the air as the warmth drew the aromatic tree essence into the atmosphere. As the holiday season peaked and the number of people using the lake went up, by the time we arrived back at the car after the swim and walk, families were flocking in, completely changing the atmosphere from what had been only a couple of hours before heavenly tranquillity. It was amazing how quickly the place could be transformed. We made a welcome escape, relieved not to be part of the lakeside crowd each day, happy to catch the best of it early for ourselves.

That first summer with Susie-Belle when we were not at the lake, we spent most of our time in the garden or at the river at the bottom of the hill. Our garden is large, steeply sloped and difficult to manage and because it lies unattended for weeks is mostly overgrown. Every year Michel valiantly battles to keep the wilderness from taking over, returning victorious to the UK only to lose all sight of success by the time he gets back a few weeks later. But he remains undeterred and good-naturedly resumes the contest, once again hacking and clearing six-foot high nettles and tangled brambles for hours on end. Renae likes to participate in any gardening, working her way up and down the garden in intense pursuit of canine horticultural happiness. After a busy afternoon helping out, she will appear from the bottom of the long garden, her beard knotted with leaves, twigs and assorted greenery; the fur on her belly thick with plump seed heads collected on her way up through the undergrowth.

Whilst Renae kept busy assisting Michel, Susie-Belle was happier quietly snoozing off the morning's lakeside exertions on her bed under the apple trees as I dozed on my lounger, keeping her company. Most days we were at the mercy of the fierce August heat by mid-afternoon when Renae and Michel would leave their garden warfare for another day, soon joining us under the fruit trees. Despite the deep shade and relative cool, Susie-Belle seemed to struggle to maintain an even level of comfort on the hottest days, with little warning she would move from gentle panting to great heaving rapid pants. I wondered at the drama of her temperature regulation, so different to Renae's moderate response, and have since seen other puppy farm dogs be similarly dramatic when hot. Maybe when they spend a lifetime suffering in extremes of temperature with no one to make it more comfortable, they learn to pre-empt the suffering by doing all they can to deal with it when they first sense it happening. Whatever Susie-Belle was thinking, she certainly made a scene of cooling herself down and as soon as I noticed her panting, I would move her into the summer house, which lay shaded by the spreading branches of a couple of large fruit trees.

Even whilst sprawled on the cold tiled floor of the summerhouse, she would have moments of dramatic panting, only to stop when I brought out her afternoon snack. I discovered purely by chance that both Susie-Belle and Renae enjoy eating melon, all types, from refreshing, crunchy slices of watermelon to juicy yellow cubes of fragrant cantaloupe. One afternoon Michel and I had been sharing an overripe honeydew and both girls had sat at our feet, staring intently as we ate slice after slice. It was clear they were keen to try it, so they did, and both guzzled each tiny piece down with an intense appreciation it would have been remiss not to reward.

So we gave them melon most days from there on: it was an ideal way to cool them down, but also provide vital hydration in the heat of the day. Most importantly it made them both very happy. After the pleasure of fresh melon, we experimented with frozen slices of ripe peach and banana and, if we had been to the morning market, their afternoon frozen fruit salad often contained sweet, fat strawberries cut into quarters. Hand feeding the sliced fruit pieces became a favourite afternoon ritual for us all.

At the bottom of our hill, the River Dronne gently meanders through the cornfields and late afternoons we often enjoy a refreshing visit during the summer. Although we can easily reach it on foot and happily do so in the spring and autumn, picking our way along the overgrown path through the fields, the hike back up the hill in high summer becomes unbearably hot, undoing any refreshment gained from our river dip. So on days when we fancied an extra dose of cool, aquatic pleasure, we popped the girls into the car and drove the long way round, past the farm, along the tree-lined lane to park up under the stone bridge as it crosses the river. Often there's not a soul around and we enjoy having the place to ourselves. At most there is only ever the odd person there, with either child or dog (or both) paddling in the shallow water. The river bed is stony and the water runs crystal-clear and shallow, not deep enough for a good swim, but perfect for a cooling dip under the thick canopy of trees providing welcoming relief from the heat of the sun.

Renae's river swimming hadn't progressed much that year and she was still reluctant to get herself wet, preferring to stand on the bank, sometimes venturing close enough for her paws to sense moisture but no more. On the hottest days Michel would carry her into the water so she could cool herself thoroughly, holding her in the water in his arms, feeling her relax. We tried to teach her to swim, supporting her under her chest, helping her to feel buoyant but she never gained the technique, instead vertically splashing her way back to the riverbank, looking as if she was trying to run on the water's surface. Her uncoordinated flapping movements created so much splashing it was hopeless trying to get her to enjoy it and in the end we gave up and let her remain watching from the bank.

On the other hand Susie-Belle continued to demonstrate her fine mastery of swimming, discovered only a couple of months earlier. She so obviously enjoyed the time we spent there together in the cool, clear water. It was ironic that her confident superior swimming style was about the only area in which she could show Renae how things should be done. The more usual pattern was for her to follow, creeping her way to normality by following her sister, but in the river she took the lead and when she had had enough and climbed up the bank to join Renae, she would roll in the dust at her feet in displays of joyous abandonment. We like to think she was sharing her love of swimming with Renae, trying to encourage her to let go of her resistance and join in. Watching her in those moments brought a deep sense of pleasure for she was not only happy herself, she was eager to share it too. Such a healthy canine response to happiness – they want to spread it wide when they feel it.

The weeks passed and all too quickly our summer sojourn drew to a close and we had to shut up the house and return to England and work. By the time we reached the end of our stay, Susie-Belle had been with us for a full year, through which time she had slowly but surely transformed into an almost normal dog. Her health was good, her eyes were responding well to the daily treatment and giving us no cause for concern. Thankfully the earlier corneal ulcer had not been a precursor of further deterioration. It felt good to know that we had been able to help her escape her pain, put it behind her and now move on with us at her side throughout the rest of her life.

CHAPTER TWENTY-THREE

Courage Rewarded

Up from a past that's rooted in pain I rise
       – 'AND STILL I RISE', MAYA ANGELOU

Shortly after we arrived back in the UK, we took Susie-Belle and Renae out to the Oxfordshire-Berkshire border to take part in the Diana Brimblecombe Animal Rescue Centre annual fundraising Fun Day. A fabulous Elizabethan mansion played host, easily accommodating the stalls, tents and rings for the dog show in its beautiful grounds. The setting was stunning – the lawns of Mapledurham House slope right down to the River Thames, providing an ideal venue with lots of room for all the activities on offer. Janet and her team of staff and volunteers had done a superb job of setting everything up and when we arrived, the site looked amazing. There were stalls selling all kinds of pet related items, from tasty treats to toys, beds and coats – anything and everything could be found somewhere on site. Right in the centre of the area, the show rings were ready and waiting for the first entrants of the day in the Fun Dog Show. This was no Crufts – the aim was to give every dog and owner the chance to have fun, not to be taken seriously and not to care in the least about winning or losing. At least that was the aim.

I will admit to being competitive by nature and making a bad job of masking this by supposedly getting behind the fundraising point of the day and entering Renae and Susie-Belle for as many of the classes in the show as I could squeeze them into. First up was Renae in the Prettiest Bitch category, where she was up against some serious competition, including an immaculately groomed Afghan Hound over on the far side of the ring who had been carried across the grass, presumably to avoid dirtying her prettily turned-out paws. By comparison I thought of my efforts the day before when I had put in a good amount of time sprucing up Renae. I gave her beard several washes and it had turned from its customary mucky ginger (courtesy of her penchant for grubbing round in the garden) to a faded ginger, which with half-closed eyes might have passed for strawberry blonde. It was the most we could manage, so before I entered the ring, I added her pretty pink collar and hoped for the best. As the judge headed over the grass towards us, I thought it would go one of two ways: Renae would either bark like crazy at him, warn he could look but not touch and forget the pretty bitch bit (she is a dog with good guarding instincts she likes to show off), or, and this was what I hoped for, she would turn on the charm and show her sweet and sensitive side, the one she reserves for special moments. And she didn't let me down – how could I have doubted her? As the judge came up, completely unprompted Renae lifted a paw for him to shake, tilted her head, looked over her shoulder at me for approval, and I could have sworn gave me a knowing wink. She was the cutest dog in the ring as far as I saw and we were happy to be only slightly beaten into second place and to go home with her first ever rosette and prize of delicious home-baked organic biscuits from Oscar's Bakery.

The day was unusually hot for mid-September and, by midday, the heat was pretty intense so we headed over towards the river for a picnic and rest. As well as the DBARC day, there was a Flyball competition event happening further up the field and the river was swarming with happy swimming collies cooling off from their morning exertions. Seeing so many dogs in the water, all merrily enjoying themselves was a great sight. I would have liked to join in their fun but it was strictly dogs only for swimming that day. I had never seen a Flyball competition before and was astounded at the energy, excitement and noise that the event created. Everyone involved, dogs and people alike, was having the most incredible if exhausting fun, adding to the brilliant atmosphere.

After a light snack and rest under the trees beside the river, we had a wander round the stalls, giving Susie-Belle a go at Temptation Alley – she had to walk along a line of sausages, ignoring them as she went, to collect a bigger, tastier prize at the end. Unsurprisingly she failed to get past the first sausage and we swiftly conceded defeat and walked on, leaving the Alley to less-greedy dogs. There were a lot of dogs of all shapes and sizes around, all getting along well. Many had spent time at DBARC, finding their new homes through the efforts of Janet and her team. It was a busy day that was a wonderful celebration of the work done by those involved with DBARC. Like the Pup Aid event a year earlier, it was a day where there were many people who understood the needs of dogs with difficult, or unknown backgrounds gathered together. Through the year with Susie-Belle I had been convinced that by sharing situations with her where she would meet friendly people and dogs, it would help her to gain confidence and learn to trust humans. At all times I had monitored how she was coping and I was very aware of the difference between flooding her with things that she may well put up with but not benefit from and the carefully managed exposure which would help to change her responses and behaviour. Seeing her wandering round in the midst of the activity, approaching new people in the moments when she felt a little more confident, I was sure that we had managed to get things right. I would have liked to have transported her back to the puppy farm just for a second, to find the people who had abused her and to make them see her now, see her as the happy, cherished family member she now was. But this would have been wasted on them for to do as they do with dogs in puppy farms, they are not humans capable of recognising the love that is possible between man and dog. They are the ones lacking, not the dogs and if they saw my wonderful dog Susie-Belle sadly it would not touch them in any way, of this I am certain.

After a wander round the stalls, we sat for a while in the shade of a gazebo, where Janet's little schnauzer Tica was taking the day quietly in her own place of safe retreat. She had been with Janet for over six months and was about to be officially adopted by her; at that stage she was still extremely nervous around people and highly touch averse. But she sat peacefully in the quiet shade of the gazebo and after a few minutes observing me came and nuzzled my hand, a small thing for most dogs but a major show of increasing confidence in a dog still largely terrified of most humans. I felt very honoured that Tica had shown me this little sign that she was slowly moving towards a more confident life. The impulse was there within her, she had shown me that – it just needed time to become her norm.

Towards the end of the afternoon, I was due back in the show ring as Susie-Belle was entered for the Dog of Courage class, a category for dogs with courageous stories to tell and of course I had entered my special girl. The award was set up in honour of one of DBARC's ex-committee members who rescued a dog that had suffered years of abuse being used as a fighting dog. When rescued, the poor dog was covered in wounds, emaciated and suffering from dreadful mange but over time his wonderful rescuer eventually nursed him back to health. Sadly he could never get him over his dog aggression but together they lived a number of years in relative peace together.

Standing in the ring with Susie-Belle at my feet (who was by this stage of the day quite hot and tired), I listened to this and other tales of the dogs we were competing against and knew that they all deserved to win. They were all dogs that had suffered in their lives, whether through cruelty inflicted by humans, or illness they had battled to overcome. Their inspirational stories showed the remarkable depths of courage and resilience that can be found in dogs and I was moved to be in the company of such true heroes. My entry for Susie-Belle was a spur-of-the-moment decision and earlier that morning I had hastily scribbled out a few words sharing my reasons for thinking her worthy of the award. As the judges read out each testament to the dogs, every single one showed they were a worthy contender, but it was our tale that won the day.

As my words were read out of how my brave, gorgeous Susie-Belle had endured so much of what is awful in life but who had the strength and courage to allow us to love and care for her, tears threatened to flow as I realised what a remarkable dog had entered our lives a year before. As the judges explained that Susie-Belle's background had left her severely damaged, I thought of how much change she had undergone in the year we had shared. She had bravely allowed us to introduce her to many new experiences and little challenges, rising to each with a grace and courage that never failed her. Not once had she objected to having endless eye drops and ointments applied, showing a level of trust and total compliance that would be rare in the most balanced and normal of dogs, let alone one unused to human care and contact. Above all, she had shown the strength of courage to accept our love. When Susie-Belle was announced the winner of the DBARC Dog of Courage award, Michel and I were without question the proudest people in the show that day and truly thankful to have her in our lives.

CHAPTER TWENTY-FOUR

Learning from Susie-Belle

'You rose into my life like a promised sunrise, brightening my days with the light in your eyes. I've never been so strong. Now I'm where I belong'

– MAYA ANGELOU

When Susie-Belle first arrived at Janet's she had never walked on a lead and most likely had never been outside in the open air for any length of time. Dogs in commercial breeding places are often kept indoors their entire lives and even those with access to the outdoors are kept confined to cages or kennels, frequently with no protection from the elements. With no shelter from wind, rain and cold, or the heat of the sun, they live in misery and it's hard to imagine what is worse: being kept indoors in narrow concrete pens never seeing the sun, or in cages stacked several high, exposed to the harshness of the outdoor environment. Puppy mills or puppy farms, or battery farms (or whatever they are called), in whatever country, are places of utter misery for the wretched creatures confined by immoral humans. It is easy for normal human beings with a trace of compassion for animals to accept that the shocking end of the spectrum of commercial dog breeding is wrong. However, commercial puppy breeding can take many forms and where the agricultural buildings, old pig pens and remodelled cattle stalls in remote locations are perhaps the most shocking and blatant examples, the people running those are far from alone in their callous approach to breeding dogs.

I know that the whole issue of dog breeding is a difficult topic and carries with it many controversies, problems and opinions. Indeed I myself remain unclear on the ethics of breeding puppies at all when the animal shelters are overflowing and millions of healthy animals are euthanised every year simply because there are too many dogs for the homes that want them... but I dearly wanted Renae and love a particular breed of dog. However, as my journey with Susie-Belle has opened my eyes to a world of suffering for so many dogs involved in breeding, there are so many caveats that should be attached to breeding that are far from ever being accepted, or the norm, that I endlessly question the morals of much of what is done today. Breeding animals should be something that only happens with a great deal of thought, research and effort but above all, compassion. In my opinion dog breeding is not all bad – far from it. Certainly there are some fair, responsible and kind dog breeders who put the health of their animals above any commercial considerations. But there are also many who don't, and when breeders care first about profitable production it is terrible and it is also unethical. Puppy farming is patently awful where intensive breeding happens and the animals are kept in horrendous conditions but there are plenty of less clearly defined examples of commercial breeding that still result in the dogs suffering. Filthy barns aren't the only places dogs suffer for commercial ends – there are those that are relatively respectable, with purpose-built facilities and kennels. Yet the dogs remain confined and bred continually and not provided with enough to meet their basic psychological and social needs. Their lives are still grim even if they are not left in their own excrement for days on end, with filth or dead puppies around them.

Dolly is an ex-breeding bitch from a commercial breeding establishment, that is far from the type of grim and nasty place that Susie-Belle inhabited, but the damage done to Dolly is of the same order. Her breeder keeps a lot of animals onsite, outside in kennels, and the operation is entirely legal and approved by official bodies. By appointment, the buying public can visit the premises, unlike the type of isolated place Susie-Belle left behind. They will see only what the breeder chooses to show them but it does allow them to claim they are open to the public. Yet the nature of the trauma experienced by the dogs there is not so different, as Dolly's story told by Bob, with whom she now lives, shows:

When my dog Flo died totally unexpectedly, two years ago, the house became horribly empty – so I wanted another dog straightaway but didn't want a puppy as I knew I had to go away for period of time. So I started wandering round the Web and found a place that had surplus-to-requirements breeding bitches (I strongly suspect that this was due to Council pressure but I have no evidence for that). I wanted a dog that would be placid enough to accompany me everywhere – which is what I got. Mainly because she was terrified of everything, all character or spirit had obviously been knocked out of her. Whenever anything new happened to her, she would instantly cower then try to flee.

When I went to see her for the first time, I took a friend who was convinced I was making a huge mistake and spent the long drive telling me so. But we went and then did exactly the wrong thing as neither my sensible friend nor I were prepared to leave her in what was clearly a pretty awful place. Dolly will never be able to go to kennels as that would put her mentally straight back there in that horrible place. Once I took a friend to collect a dog from the local animal sanctuary and Dolly came with us. The moment she heard the barking, she fled, cowering into the car, and refused to come out for anything.

She had obviously had little or no human contact and didn't respond to her name, although the breeder had told me it – probably for appearance's sake rather than being helpful. Dolly had never had a rawhide chew – the first one I gave her, I had to hold it in her mouth till she realised she was expected to chew on it.

She wasn't house trained and it takes quite a while to house train a five-year-old. In fact, she was completely undomesticated. She had clearly never seen stairs. At first, when we were out she was always so close to me that there were claw marks on my heels – she hated having anyone or any dog behind her. Not surprising really in a breeding bitch. It took many months of regular socialisation before she'd go more than a few feet from me. She still strongly prefers women to men and will more readily come to my female friends than to me. She is just beginning to be able to play nearly two years later but is easily discouraged. She

clearly wants to play, but isn't sure how. I have only once
seen her do the play bow and when another dog does it to
her, she's as likely to submit as join in.

Whilst many puppy farms are illegal and should be closed
down, but aren't, there are plenty that operate within the law
with locally issued licenses. Dolly was unwanted, or worn-out,
breeding 'stock' from a legitimate, licensed business that is
operating perfectly legally and openly. When no longer useful,
her breeders made sure to get every last penny from her: they
sold her to Bob. If their methods or motives were challenged,
they would no doubt claim that they gave her sufficient care
throughout her life, praise her as a much-loved member of
their family and yet pass her on to whoever comes along with
the money when they decide she is no longer required. To hear
the similarities between her behavioural and emotional issues
and those of Susie-Belle is striking. It is impossible to ignore
the fact that commercial breeding on a scale where the dogs
are not living in the home and given ample, not minimal,
human contact is just plain wrong. Moreover, that contact
should not be cursory, it should be loving, genuine contact.
Dogs are not like other animals – they are not, and never in
the vastness of human or canine history have been, commonly
used as livestock. It feels instinctively wrong to treat
companion animals in the same way as livestock animals.

Our relationship with dogs is a unique one that predates all
other domesticated species by a long way. Recent academic
study discussed beautifully in Jeffrey Moussaieff Masson's
elegant book, *The Dog Who Couldn't Stop Loving* shows that we
coevolved, a process that gave rise to an intimacy not known
in other species and which those living with dogs today will
surely recognise. Dogs are special animals that need

affectionate contact with people but they don't just enjoy it, they absolutely need it in order to thrive. Humans and dogs are the only creatures that consistently, by default, form relationships and demonstrate real friendships with other species, with each other. Occasionally other animals may do it – elephants have been known to make relationships across the species barrier – but people and dogs are the only two that consistently do it, according to Masson. Other animals do not show this capacity. Dogs do it by their very nature and must suffer terribly when humans abuse them or do not love or care for them. It must be utterly bewildering for breeding dogs to be left alone, bereft of human friendship year after year, even if their basic physical needs are met.

In the UK, although councils are required to inspect the premises of all breeding establishments there are documented cases of terrible conditions being found in licensed premises which go unremarked, or unnoticed until many animals suffer a terrible plight. It is questionable how these inspections are done. Regulations do exist in the UK and other countries like the US and Australia that should prevent a lot of the abuse that happens in commercial breeding, but they are not enforced, allowing the misery to continue for millions of dogs and their puppies around the world.

Puppy farms produce and sell all kinds of dog, including purebreeds as well as fashionable designer crossbreeds. Whatever is profitable will be bred, for this is plain and simply a business. It has nothing to do with maintaining breed standards, or preventing breed related illnesses – Susie-Belle's cataracts, Tica's progressive retinal atrophy and all their puppies who will go on to develop these problems are testament to that.

When I have told people about Susie-Belle's story and

background, many have been upset and disturbed to know such appalling conditions exist in Britain. Often I am asked how they are legal and why they are not closed down. I cannot answer those questions without feeling extreme anger and frustration. From what I see, regulations and laws do exist that should prevent suffering but animals continue to suffer and the ease with which breeders can sell their puppies makes the situation even bleaker. A distinguishing feature of responsible breeders is to whom they will sell their puppies. A responsible breeder takes care to ensure the puppies go to good homes and does all he can to support the new owners and offer lifetime support. A good breeder genuinely cares what life puppies have, whereas a commercially driven breeder will sell to anyone. The object is to produce and sell puppies, as many as possible to maximise profits. The stereotypical puppy farmer will not allow anyone to see the place where the dogs are bred – they either sell to dealers or they have a respectable house to act as their 'shop front' from which they sell the dogs themselves. In between, there are commercial breeders blurring the line – there are plenty of places like the one where Dolly lived out her first few years.

The internet has made puppy dealing easy and profitable and supplies the demand that keeps the puppy farmers in business. The fad for designer breeds multiplies the misery. Frequently puppies advertised on internet sites are sourced from hellish puppy farms. As long as the demand for puppies continues to exist, I fear that puppy farms will continue to operate until the buying public are better educated.

Whilst it may be desirable that everyone wanting a dog would adopt one who needs a home this is never going to happen. Educating the puppy buying public and encouraging as many people as possible to adopt from shelters and rescues is more realistic. If more people do their homework and research exactly what having a dog entails, what breed suits their lifestyle and not just what breed they fancy, this may go some way towards improving the welfare of dogs. I believe that dog breeding is only acceptable when it is not done for commercial ends, and that the animals involved are living in a normal home environment, like the companion animals they are. People should know that when they buy a puppy, they must look to see what conditions the mother and litter are living in and they should be together. A puppy should not be kept away from its mother until it leaves to start a new life in a loving, caring home.

Anyone with any awareness of this topic should speak out about it, tell friends, families and acquaintances about puppy farming – educate people about buying puppies responsibly. Until more people know to avoid internet sales of puppies and any third party seller, there will be a constant demand to satisfy. Every organisation and local authority with any responsibility must use their powers to enforce the animal welfare regulations that exist. They should be lobbied and made to address the abuse they turn a blind eye to. Only when we all take responsibility for this will anything change for the dogs who continue to suffer but who just want to love and be loved by humans.

Many people say to me that Susie-Belle is a very lucky dog to have the life she now does – to go from having no home to having two comfortable homes, to travel and holiday as often as she does, to eat the foods she enjoys, to be safe and loved, but I always feel awkward with this sentiment, although I do understand what is meant. My sense of unease at considering her lucky comes from recognising that although she is lucky in the sense she is now free from the torture of her previous life and was one of those fortunate enough to survive long enough to be rescued and to live freely, she is only living the way that dogs should live and being loved as all dogs should be loved. Renae shares the same pleasures and unlike Susie-Belle has not had to earn them a million times over so in that respect my darling dog is not lucky. She deserves all she now has. It seems churlish when I want to bat away well-intentioned comments about her current good fortune but in my heart, I know that she brings me as much pleasure as I know her life now gives her and as she has grown, I too have grown.

Yet if we are bold,
love strikes away the chains of fear
from our souls.
– 'TOUCHED BY AN ANGEL', *MAYA ANGELOU*

Acknowledgements

This book has been inspired by the work of all who dedicate themselves to animal rescue but particularly those who concentrate their efforts on ending the battery farming of dogs. I thank all who have taken an interest in Susie-Belle's journey and helped us on it. They are many and include several four-legged friends who have contributed to her healing in a myriad of ways, some obvious, many less so but all immensely valuable.

Most special thanks to Janet, Susie-Belle's foster mum, who not only gave her the love and care she needed in the first months of her new life out of the puppy farm, but who trusted me enough to adopt our special girl. Janet remains my inspiration. All the staff and volunteers at the Diana Brimblecombe Animal Rescue Centre who do so much excellent work, but particularly Donna for her foster work and Bethany for being the kind of young person the world of animal rescue needs. Kathleen, a true friend with whom I regularly share black humour and much laughter – we have to laugh over our dogs' problems, few others would. Kate, with her enthusiasm for finding, sharing and joining walks, and letting Renae amuse herself by keeping Rodders entertained; Dean and Jolyon, who have travelled much of our journey with us, shared so much, including camping gear, plentiful food and wine and the company of Rupert and Watson. Ace amateur photographer Mike Jackson who has taken the most stunning photographs of Susie-Belle and Renae, capturing forever their personalities, with skills rarely seen in professionals. Zoe, a good friend who runs marathons for fun, fund-raises, gives Bella the wonderful life she now lives and makes me worry a lot less about my own competitiveness. My wonderful friend Emma for her timely, imaginative encouragement when I was struggling to find the words I needed to say. Members of the UK Schnauzer Forum, some of whom we have met in real life and many we haven't, for sharing support and stories. Everyone that has shared their experiences and allowed me to use them here has strengthened my resolve to do anything I can to end puppy farming and I applaud every single person who opens their home and heart to one of these special dogs. I have also been very grateful to Leigh for sharing her thoughts on a difficult topic and helping me to grapple with it and to find clarity from the muddle of my thoughts.

To all the people who go into the hellholes that are the battery farms that confine dogs like Susie-Belle, and take them away to their new lives, who time and again see first-hand the horrors, the suffering, the inhumanity, I have a profound admiration for their courage to continue their work. Finally, to the nameless individual who found her, I thank you for bringing out Susie-Belle.

CHAPTER ONE

Further Reading and Information

I have found the following books very helpful in deepening my understanding of canine psychology and how this can help me to improve our lives together and I highly recommend them:

Bradshaw, John. *In Defence of Dogs: Why Dogs Need Our Understanding* (Penguin, 2012).
Hare, Brian and Woods, Vanessa. *The Genius of Dogs: Discovering the Unique Intelligence of Man's Best Friend* (Oneworld Publications, 2013).
Horowitz, Alexandra. *Inside of a Dog: What Dogs See, Smell and Know* (Simon & Schuster Ltd., 2009).
Moussaieff Masson, Jeffrey. *Dogs Never Lie About Love: Why Your Dog Will Always Love You More Than Anyone Else: Reflections on the Emotional World of Dogs* (Vintage, 1998).
— *The Dog Who Couldn't Stop Loving: How Dogs Have*

Captured Our Hearts for Thousands of Years
(HarperPaperbacks, 2011).

Researching canine nutrition I continue to read a lot, discard
much and often return to these sources for information:
Brown, Steve. *Unlocking the Canine Ancestral Diet: healthier
dog food the ABC way* (Dogwise Publishing, 2010).
Lonsdale, Tom. *Work Wonders: feed your dog raw meaty bones*
(Rivetco, 2005).
Olson, Lew. *Raw & Natural Nutrition for Dogs: the definitive
guide to homemade meals* (North Atlantic Books, 2010).
Taylor, Beth and Shaw Becker, Karen. *Real Food for Healthy
Dogs and Cats. 4th ed.* (Natural Pet Productions, 2013).

Lew Olson's blog/newsletter:
http://www.b-naturals.com/newsletter/
Raw Food Vets: http://www.rawfoodvets.com

Organisations and individuals working to help end the
battery farming of puppies and to rescue and rehabilitate its
victims:

UK
Friends of the Animals RCT, 23 Church Road, Ton Pentre,
Rhondda Cynon Taf, CF41 7EB
http://www.friendsoftheanimalsrct.org.uk
Hope Rescue: http://www.hoperescue.org.uk
Many Tears Animal Rescue, Cwmlogin House, Cefneithin,
Llanelli, Carmarthenshire, SA14 7HB
http://www.manytearsrescue.org
Diana Brimblecombe Animal Rescue Centre, Nelsons Lane,
Hurst, Wokingham, RG10 ORR

FURTHER READING AND INFORMATION

http://www.dbarc.org.uk
Pup Aid http://www.pupaid.org
Puppy Love Campaigns http://www.puppylovecampaigns.org
Cariad Campaign, PO Box 60, Lampeter, SA48 9BE
http://cariadcampaign.wordpress.com/
Montgomery Voice for Animals, http://www.mvfa.org.uk

US
National Mill Dog Rescue, http://www.milldogrescue.org
Based in Colorado this organisation, through rescue and
education, hopes to end the cruelty of commercial puppy
breeding. I have found their work, stories and dedication
completely inspirational.